Cisco Networking Academy Program
CCNA 3 and 4 Engineering Journal and Workbook
Third Edition

Cisco Systems, Inc.
Cisco Networking Academy Program

Cisco Press

201 West 103rd Street
Indianapolis, IN 46290 USA

**Cisco Networking Academy Program
CCNA 3 and 4 Engineering Journal and Workbook, Third Edition**

Cisco Systems, Inc.

Cisco Networking Academy Program

Copyright © 2003 Cisco Systems, Inc.

Cisco Press logo is a trademark of Cisco Systems, Inc.

Published by:
Cisco Press
201 West 103rd Street
Indianapolis, IN 46290 USA

Printed in the United States of America   1 2 3 4 5 6 7 8 9 0

First Printing June 2003

ISBN: 1-58713-115-3

Trademark Acknowledgments

CISCO SYSTEMS

This book is part of the Cisco Networking Academy® Program series from Cisco Press. The products in this series support and complement the Cisco Networking Academy Program curriculum. If you are using this book outside the Networking Academy program, then you are not preparing with a Cisco trained and authorized Networking Academy provider.

For information on the Cisco Networking Academy Program or to locate a Networking Academy, please visit www.cisco.com/edu.

Warning and Disclaimer

This book is designed to provide information on networking fundamentals. Every effort has been made to make this book as complete and accurate as possible, but no warranty or fitness is implied.

Feedback Information

At Cisco Press, our goal is to create in-depth technical books of the highest quality and value. Each book is crafted with care and precision, undergoing rigorous development that involves the unique expertise of members of the professional technical community.

Reader feedback is a natural continuation of this process. If you have any comments about how we could improve the quality of this book, or otherwise alter it to better suit your needs, you can contact us at networkingacademy@ciscopress.com. Please be sure to include the book title and ISBN in your message.

We greatly appreciate your assistance.

Publisher	**John Wait**
Editor-in-Chief	**John Kane**
Executive Editor	**Carl Lindholm**
Cisco Systems Representative	**Anthony Wolfenden**
Cisco Press Program Manager	**Sonia Torres Chavez**
Manager, Marketing Communications, Cisco Systems	**Scott Miller**
Cisco Marketing Program Manager	**Edie Quiroz**
Technical Editors	**Thomas Moffses**
	John Sirmon
Production Manager	**Patrick Kanouse**
Senior Development Editor	**Christopher Cleveland**
Senior Project Editor	**Sheri Cain**
Assistant Editor	**Sarah Kimberly**
Copy Editor	**Gayle Johnson**

CISCO SYSTEMS

Corporate Headquarters
Cisco Systems, Inc.
170 West Tasman Drive
San Jose, CA 95134-1706
USA
www.cisco.com
Tel: 408 526-4000
800 553-NETS (6387)
Fax: 408 526-4100

European Headquarters
Cisco Systems International BV
Haarlerbergpark
Haarlerbergweg 13-19
1101 CH Amsterdam
The Netherlands
www-europe.cisco.com
Tel: 31 0 20 357 1000
Fax: 31 0 20 357 1100

Americas Headquarters
Cisco Systems, Inc.
170 West Tasman Drive
San Jose, CA 95134-1706
USA
www.cisco.com
Tel: 408 526-7660
Fax: 408 527-0883

Asia Pacific Headquarters
Cisco Systems, Inc.
Capital Tower
168 Robinson Road
#22-01 to #29-01
Singapore 068912
www.cisco.com
Tel: +65 6317 7777
Fax: +65 6317 7799

Cisco Systems has more than 200 offices in the following countries and regions. Addresses, phone numbers, and fax numbers are listed on the
Cisco.com Web site at www.cisco.com/go/offices.

Argentina • Australia • Austria • Belgium • Brazil • Bulgaria • Canada • Chile • China PRC • Colombia • Costa Rica • Croatia • Czech Republic
Denmark • Dubai, UAE • Finland • France • Germany • Greece • Hong Kong SAR • Hungary • India • Indonesia • Ireland • Israel • Italy
Japan • Korea • Luxembourg • Malaysia • Mexico • The Netherlands • New Zealand • Norway • Peru • Philippines • Poland • Portugal
Puerto Rico • Romania • Russia • Saudi Arabia • Scotland • Singapore • Slovakia • Slovenia • South Africa • Spain • Sweden
Switzerland • Taiwan • Thailand • Turkey • Ukraine • United Kingdom • United States • Venezuela • Vietnam • Zimbabwe

Table of Contents

Preface

Since 1997, the Cisco Networking Academy Program has instituted an e-learning model that integrates the multimedia delivery of a networking curriculum with testing, performance-based skills assessment, evaluation, and reporting through a web interface. The Cisco Networking Academy Program curriculum goes beyond traditional computer-based instruction by helping students develop practical networking knowledge and skills in a hands-on environment. In a lab setting that closely corresponds to a real networking environment, students work with the architecture and infrastructure pieces of networking technology. As a result, they learn the principles and practices of networking technology.

The Cisco Networking Academy Program provides in-depth and meaningful networking content. Regional and Local Academies teach students around the world by using the curriculum to integrate networking instruction into the classroom. The focus of the Networking Academy program is the integration of a web-based network curriculum into the learning environment. This element is addressed through intensive staff development for instructors and innovative classroom materials and approaches to instruction, which Cisco provides. Participating educators receive resources, remote access to online support, and the knowledge base for the effective integration of the Networking Academy curriculum into the classroom learning environment. As a result, the Networking Academy program enables the dynamic exchange of information by providing a suite of services that redefine how instructional resources are disseminated, resulting in a many-to-many interactive and collaborative network of teachers and students functioning to meet diverse educational needs.

The Networking Academy curriculum is especially exciting for educators and students because the courseware is interactive. Because of the growing use of interactive technologies, the curriculum is a way to convey instruction with new interactive technologies that allow instructors and trainers to mix a number of media, including audio, video, text, numerical data, and graphics. Consequently, students can select different media from the computer screen and tweak the instructional content to meet their needs, and educators can either design their own environment for assessment or choose an assessment.

Finally, by developing a curriculum that recognizes changing classroom and workforce demographics, the globalization of the economy, changing workforce knowledge and skill requirements, and the role of technology in education, the Cisco Networking Academy Program supports national educational goals for K-12 education. To support the Networking Academy program, Cisco Press published this book as a further complement to the curriculum used in the Cisco Networking Academy Program.

Foreword

Throughout the world, the Internet has brought tremendous new opportunities for individuals and their employers. Companies and other organizations are seeing dramatic increases in productivity by investing in robust networking capabilities. Some studies have shown measurable productivity improvements in entire economies. The promise of enhanced efficiency, profitability, and standard of living is real and growing.

Such productivity gains aren't achieved by simply purchasing networking equipment. Skilled professionals are needed to plan, design, install, deploy, configure, operate, maintain, and troubleshoot today's networks. Network managers need to assure that they've planned for network security and for continued operation. They need to design for the performance level required in their organization. They need to implement new capabilities as the demands of their organization, and its reliance on the network, expands.

To meet the many educational needs of the internetworking community, Cisco established the Cisco Networking Academy Program. The Cisco Networking Academy Program is a comprehensive learning program that provides students with the Internet technology skills essential in a global economy. The Networking Academy program integrates face-to-face teaching, web-based content, online assessment, student performance tracking, hands-on labs, instructor training and support, and preparation for industry-standard certifications.

The Networking Academy program continually raises the bar on blended learning and educational processes. The Internet-based assessment and instructor support systems are some of the most extensive and validated ever developed, including a 24/7 customer service system for Academy instructors. Through community feedback and electronic assessment, the Networking Academy program adapts curriculum to improve outcomes and student achievement. The Cisco Global Learning Network infrastructure designed for the Networking Academy program delivers a rich, interactive, and personalized curriculum to students around the world. The Internet has the power to change the way people work, live, play and learn, and the Cisco Networking Academy Program is in the forefront of this transformation.

This Cisco Press title is one of a series of best-selling companion titles for the Cisco Networking Academy Program. These books are designed by Cisco Worldwide Education and Cisco Press to provide integrated support for the online learning content that is made available to Academies all over the world. These Cisco Press books are the only books authorized for the Academy program by Cisco Systems, and provide print and CD-ROM materials that help ensure the greatest possible learning experience for Networking Academy students.

I hope you are successful as you embark on your learning path with Cisco and the Internet. I also hope that you'll choose to continue your learning after you complete the Academy curriculum. In addition to its Cisco Networking Academy titles, Cisco Press also publishes an extensive list of networking technology and certification publications that provide a wide range of resources. Cisco has also established a network of professional training companies—the Cisco Learning Partners—who provide a full range of Cisco training courses. They offer training in many formats, including e-learning, self-paced, and instructor-led classes. Their instructors are certified by Cisco, and their materials are created

by Cisco. When you're ready, please visit the Learning & Events area on www.cisco.com to learn about all the educational support that Cisco and its partners have to offer.

Thank you for choosing this book and the Cisco Networking Academy Program.

Kevin Warner

Senior Director, Marketing

Worldwide Education

Cisco Systems, Inc.

Introduction

This book is a supplement to your classroom and laboratory experience with the Cisco Networking Academy Program, whose curriculum is designed to empower you to enter employment or further your education and training in the computer networking field.

This book is designed to train you beyond the online training materials you have already used in this program, along with the topics pertaining to the Cisco Certified Network Associate (CCNA) exam. This book closely follows the style and format that Cisco has incorporated into the curriculum. This book gives you additional exercises and activities that reinforce your learning. Also included are writing opportunities that help you learn to establish and keep an engineering journal. We recommend that you keep a technical, or engineering journal. Typically, a journal is a paperbound composition book in which pages are not added or subtracted, but dated. The types of journal entries most applicable for Networking Academy students include daily reflections, troubleshooting details, lab procedures and observations, equipment logs, hardware and software notes, and router configurations. Your journal becomes more important as you do more network design and installations, so you can develop good habits by starting a journal the first day of CCNA 3.0. In this book, you are asked to keep your journal on a daily basis.

Chapter 1

Review: The OSI Reference Model and Routing

Networks are complex environments that involve multiple media, protocols, and interconnections to networks outside an organization's central office. Well-designed and carefully installed networks can reduce the problems associated with growth as a networking environment evolves.

Designing, building, and maintaining a network can be a challenging task. Even a small network that consists of only 50 nodes can pose complex problems that lead to unpredictable results. Large networks that feature thousands of nodes can pose even more complex problems. Despite improvements in equipment performance and media capabilities, designing and building a network is difficult.

This chapter reviews the Open Systems Interconnection (OSI) reference model and provides an overview of network planning and design considerations related to routing. Much of this information should be familiar, because you were introduced to these concepts in the first year of the Cisco Networking Academy Program. Using the OSI reference model as a reference for network design can facilitate changes. Using the OSI reference model as a hierarchical structure for network design lets you design networks in layers. The OSI reference model is at the heart of building and designing networks, with every layer performing a specific task to promote data communications. In the world of networking, Layers 1 through 4 are the focus. These four layers define the following:

- The type and speed of LAN and WAN media to be implemented
- How data is sent across the media
- The type of addressing schemes used
- How data is reliably sent across the network and how flow control is accomplished
- The type of routing protocol implemented

Concept Questions

Demonstrate your knowledge of these concepts by answering the following questions in the space provided.

1. By using layers, the OSI model simplifies the task required for two computers to communicate. Explain why.

_____

_____

2. Each layer's protocol exchanges information, called protocol data units (PDUs), between peer layers. Explain how this is done.

_____

_____

_____

_____

3. Explain the concept of encapsulation.

_____

_____

_____

_____

4. Explain what the term *Ethernet* means.

_____

_____

_____

5. What is a datagram?

_____

_____

6. What is ARP, and how does it work?

_____

_____

_____

_____

7. Most routing protocols can be classified as one of two basic types: routed or routing. What are the differences between the two?

_____

_____

_____

_____

8. Examples of IP routing protocols include RIP, IGRP, OSPF, and EIGRP. Explain the differences between these different types of protocols.

_____

_____

_____

_____

Vocabulary Exercise

Define the following terms as completely as you can. Use the online curriculum or Chapter 1 of the *Cisco Networking Academy Program CCNA 3 and 4 Companion Guide*, Third Edition, for help.

application layer

_____

_____

_____

ARP

_____

_____

_____

Cisco IOS Software

_____

_____

_____

datagram

_____

_____

_____

data link layer

_____

_____

_____

default route

_____

_____

_____

distance vector routing protocol

_____

_____

_____

dynamic routing

_____

_____

_____

EIGRP

_____

_____

_____

flow control

_____

_____

_____

ICMP

_____

_____

_____

IGRP

_____

_____

_____

IP address

_____

_____

_____

MAC

_____

_____

_____

network

_____

_____

_____

network layer

_____

_____

_____

NIC

_____

_____

_____

packet

_____

_____

_____

presentation layer

_____

_____

_____

RARP

_____

_____

_____

SPF

_____

_____

_____

static routing

_____

_____

_____

stub network

_____

_____

_____

Focus Questions

1. List each of the layers of the OSI model and identify their functions. Indicate what networking and internetworking devices operate at each layer. Be specific.

_____

_____

_____

_____

_____

_____

_____

_____

_____

_____

_____

_____

_____

_____

_____

_____

_____

_____

2.   Outline a presentation that you might give to your parents that explains the OSI model. What examples might you use?

   _____

   _____

   _____

   _____

   _____

CCNA Exam Review Questions

The following questions help you review for the CCNA exam. The answers appear in Appendix A, "Answers to CCNA Exam Review Questions."

1. Which OSI layer supports file transfer?

   A. Application layer

   B. Network layer

   C. Presentation layer

   D. Session layer

   E. Physical layer

2. Which OSI layer negotiates data transfer syntax such as ASCII?

   A. Network layer

   B. Transport layer

   C. Application layer

   D. Physical layer

   E. Presentation layer

3. Which OSI layer deals with connection coordination between applications?

   A. Physical layer

   B. Data link layer

   C. Transport layer

   D. Session layer

   E. Presentation layer

4. Which OSI layer supports reliable connections for data transport services?

   A. Application layer

   B. Session layer

   C. Presentation layer

   D. Physical layer

   E. Transport layer

5.   At what layer does routing occur?

    A.   Session layer

    B.   Application layer

    C.   Network layer

    D.   Transport layer

    E.   Data link layer

Chapter 2

Introduction to Classless Routing

This chapter introduces classless routing, classless interdomain routing (CIDR), variable-length subnet mask (VLSM), and Routing Information Protocol version 2 (RIPv2).

With the explosive growth of IP networks, most importantly the global Internet, the available IP address space was shrinking, and the core Internet routers were running out of capacity. CIDR was developed to address these problems.

CIDR replaced the old process of assigning IP addresses based on Class A, B, and C addresses with a generalized network prefix. Instead of being limited to network identifiers (or prefixes) of 8, 16, or 24 bits, CIDR currently uses prefixes anywhere from 13 to 27 bits. Blocks of addresses can be assigned to networks as small as 32 hosts or to those with more than 500,000 hosts. This allows for address assignments that more closely fit an organization's specific needs.

With CIDR, IP address notation changed a bit. A CIDR address includes the standard 32-bit IP address and also information on how many bits are used for the network prefix. For example, in the CIDR address 206.13.01.48/25, the /25 indicates that the first 25 bits are used to identify the unique network, leaving the remaining bits to identify the specific host. 206.13.01.48/25 can also be written as 206.13.01.48 255.255.255.128.

Concept Questions

Demonstrate your knowledge of these concepts by answering the following questions in the space provided.

1. What are some reasons for using CIDR to assign IP addresses?

   _____

   _____

   _____

   _____

2. By using a prefix address to summarize routes, you can keep routing table entries manageable. This results in what benefits?

   _____

   _____

3. What is supernetting, and how does it help?

   _____

   _____

   _____

   _____

4.   What purposes were VLSMs developed for?

_____

_____

_____

_____

5.   Provide an example of how an administrator using VLSMs can save IP addresses by further subnetting the address (172.16.32.0/20) after it has already been subnetted to a network that has only ten hosts.

_____

_____

_____

_____

6.   RIP-1 and IGRP, common interior gateway protocols, cannot support VLSM methods to determine an address's network prefix. How do these protocols determine an address's network prefix?

_____

_____

_____

_____

Vocabulary Exercise

Define the following terms as completely as you can. Use the online curriculum or Chapter 2 of the *Cisco Networking Academy Program CCNA 3 and 4 Companion Guide*, Third Edition, for help.

bitmask

_____

_____

_____

CIDR

_____

_____

_____

route summarization

_____

_____

_____

subnetting

_____

_____

_____

supernetting

_____

_____

_____

VLSM

_____

_____

_____

Focus Questions

1.   Which two of the following addresses are valid subnet addresses when
     172.17.15.0/24 is subnetted an additional 4 bits? (Choose two.)

     A.   172.17.15.0

     B.   172.17.15.8

     C.   172.17.15.40

     D.   172.17.15.96

     E.   172.17.15.248

2.   What is the most efficient subnet mask to use on point-to-point WAN links?

     A.   255.255.255.0

     B.   255.255.255.224

     C.   255.255.255.252

     D.   255.255.255.255

3.   Which of the following is a feature of CIDR?

     A.   Classful addressing

     B.   No supernetting

     C.   More entries in the routing table

     D.   Route aggregation

4. Which of the following is a summarization address for the networks 172.21.136.0/24 and 172.21.143.0/24?

    A. 172.21.136.0/21

    B. 172.21.136.0/20

    C. 172.21.136.0/22

    D. 172.21.128.0/2

5. Which of the following routing protocols does not contain subnet mask information in its routing updates?

    A. EIGRP

    B. OSPF

    C. RIPv1

    D. RIPv2

6. Which of the following methods is used to represent a collection of IP addresses with a single IP address?

    A. Classful routing

    B. Subnetting

    C. Address translation

    D. Route summarization

CCNA Exam Review Questions

The following questions help you review for the CCNA exam. The answers appear in Appendix A, "Answers to CCNA Exam Review Questions."

1. How many bits are in an IP address?

    A. 16

    B. 32

    C. 64

    D. None of the above

2. What is the maximum value of each octet in an IP address?

    A. 128

    B. 255

    C. 256

    D. None of the above

3. The network number plays what part in an IP address?

    A. It specifies the network to which the host belongs.

    B. It specifies the identity of the computer on the network.

    C. It specifies which node on the subnetwork is being addressed.

    D. It specifies which networks the device can communicate with.

4. The host number plays what part in an IP address?

    A. It designates the identity of the computer on the network.

    B. It designates which node on the subnetwork is being addressed.

    C. It designates the network to which the host belongs.

    D. It designates which hosts the device can communicate with.

5. What is the decimal equivalent to the binary number 00101101?

    A. 32

    B. 35

    C. 45

    D. 44

6. Convert the decimal number 192.5.34.11 to its binary form.

   A. 11000000.00000101.00100010.00001011

   B. 11000101.01010111.00011000.10111000

   C. 01001011.10010011.00111001.00110111

   D. 11000000.00001010.01000010.00001011

7. Convert the binary IP address 1000000.00000101.00100010.00001011 to its decimal form.

   A. 190.4.34.11

   B. 192.4.34.10

   C. 192.4.32.11

   D. None of the above

8. What portion of the Class B address 154.19.2.7 is the network address?

   A. 154

   B. 154.19

   C. 154.19.2

   D. 154.19.2.7

9. Which portion of the IP address 129.219.51.18 represents the network?

   A. 129.219

   B. 129

   C. 129.219.51.0

   D. 129.219.0.0

10. Which of the following addresses is an example of a broadcast address on the network 123.10.0.0 with a subnet mask of 255.255.0.0?

    A. 123.255.255.255

    B. 123.10.255.255

    C. 123.13.0.0

    D. 123.1.1.1

11. How many host addresses can be used in a Class C network?

    A. 253

    B. 254

    C. 255

    D. 256

12. How many subnets can a Class B network have?

    A. 16

    B. 256

    C. 128

    D. None of the above

13. What is the minimum number of bits that can be borrowed to form a subnet?

    A. 1

    B. 2

    C. 4

    D. None of the above

14. What is the primary reason for using subnets?

    A. To reduce the size of the collision domain

    B. To increase the number of host addresses

    C. To reduce the size of the broadcast domain

    D. None of the above

15. How many bits are in a subnet mask?

    A. 16

    B. 32

    C. 64

    D. None of the above

16. Performing the Boolean function as a router would on the IP addresses 131.8.2.5 *and* 255.0.0.0, what is the network/subnetwork address?

    A. 131.8.1.0

    B. 131.8.0.0

    C. 131.8.2.0

    D. None of the above

17. What is the minimum number of bits that can be borrowed to create a subnet for a Class C network?

    A.   2

    B.   4

    C.   6

    D.   None of the above

18. With a Class C address of 197.15.22.31 and a subnet mask of 255.255.255.224, how many bits have been borrowed to create a subnet?

    A.   1

    B.   2

    C.   3

    D.   None of the above

19. Performing the Boolean function as a router would on the IP addresses 172.16.2.120 *and* 255.255.255.0, what is the subnet address?

    A.   172.0.0.0

    B.   172.16.0.0

    C.   172.16.2.0

    D.   None of the above

Chapter 3

Single-Area OSPF

Link-state routing protocols differ from distance vector protocols. Link-state protocols flood link-state information and thus give every router a complete view of the network topology. With a distance vector protocol, routers do not learn about the complete network topology. Open Shortest Path First (OSPF) is a link-state protocol.

In OSPF, the shortest path first (SPF) algorithm, discovered by the computer scientist Dijkstra, is used to determine the best path – the lowest-cost path to a link.

The SPF algorithm was conceived as an algorithm for point-to-point network connections. To implement OSPF on the variety of networks that are available today, OSPF must be aware of the network type in which it operates. This allows OSPF to work correctly for these different network types.

Before link-state information is exchanged, the OSPF protocol establishes a neighbor relationship between routers. The OSPF Hello protocol is used for this purpose.

OSPF is a complex protocol and is described by a set of operational steps.

OSPF is a link-state routing protocol based on open standards. It is described in several standards of the Internet Engineering Task Force (IETF); the most recent is RFC 2328.

The Open in OSPF means that it is open to the public and is nonproprietary. OSPF is becoming the preferred IGP protocol compared to the Routing Information Protocol (RIP) because it is scalable.

RIP cannot scale beyond 15 hops, it converges slowly, and it can choose slow routes because it ignores critical factors such as bandwidth in route determination.

OSPF deals with these limitations and has been proven to be a robust, scalable routing protocol suitable for modern networks. OSPF can be used for large networks because it scales to larger networks if hierarchical network design principles are used. OSPF can also be used and configured as a single area for small networks.

OSPF can be used for large networks. OSPF routing scales to large networks if hierarchical network design principles are used.

Large OSPF networks use hierarchical design principles. Multiple areas connect to a distribution area, area 0, also called the backbone. This design approach allows for extensive control of routing updates. Defining areas reduces routing overhead, speeds up convergence, confines network instability to an area, and improves performance.

Concept Questions

Demonstrate your knowledge of these concepts by answering the following questions in the space provided.

1. As a link-state protocol, how does OSPF operate differently from distance vector routing protocols?

   _____
   _____
   _____
   _____
   _____
   _____

2. OSPF routers establish relationships, or states, with their neighbors to efficiently share link-state information. Fill in the following chart with descriptions of the different OSPF router states given the type of packet that is sent.

OSPF Packet Type	Description
Type 1 – Hello	
Type 2 – Database description packet (DBD)	
Type 3 – Link-state request	
Type 4 – Link-state update (LSU)	
Type 5 – Link-state acknowledgment (LSACK)	

3. OSPF interfaces can be in one of seven states. OSPF neighbor relationships progress through these states, one at a time, in this order:

   Down
   Init
   Two-way
   Exstart
   Exchange
   Loading
   Full adjacency

   Describe what occurs in each of these states.

   _____
   _____
   _____
   _____
   _____
   _____
   _____
   _____
   _____
   _____

_____

_____

_____

_____

_____

_____

_____

_____

_____

_____

_____

_____

_____

Vocabulary Exercise

Define the following terms as completely as you can. Use the online curriculum or Chapter 3 of the *Cisco Networking Academy Program CCNA 3 and 4 Companion Guide*, Third Edition, for help.

backbone

_____

_____

_____

BDR

_____

_____

_____

DR

_____

_____

_____

flooding

_____

_____

_____

Hello protocol

_____

_____

_____

LSA

_____

_____

_____

process identifier

_____

_____

_____

Router ID

_____

_____

_____

SPF algorithm

_____

_____

_____

Focus Questions

1. Link-state routers maintain a common picture of the network and exchange link information upon initial _____ or _____. Link-state routers do not broadcast their routing tables _____, like distance vector routing protocols do.

2. Whereas _____ is appropriate for small networks, _____ was written to address the needs of large _____ internetworks.

3. An issue OSPF addresses is speed of _____. With OSPF, _____ is faster because only the routing changes (not the entire routing table) are flooded rapidly to other routers in the OSPF network.

4. RIP broadcasts full routing tables to all neighbors every _____ seconds. However, this is especially problematic over slow WAN links, because these updates consume large amounts of bandwidth. Alternatively, OSPF _____ minimally sized link-state updates and sends the updates only when a _____ is in the network.

5. In contrast, OSPF selects optimal routes using _____ as a factor. (This is a metric based on bandwidth.)

6. List the OSPF network type that matches each topology shown in Figure 3-1.

Figure 3-1   List the OSPF Network Type

_____   _____   _____

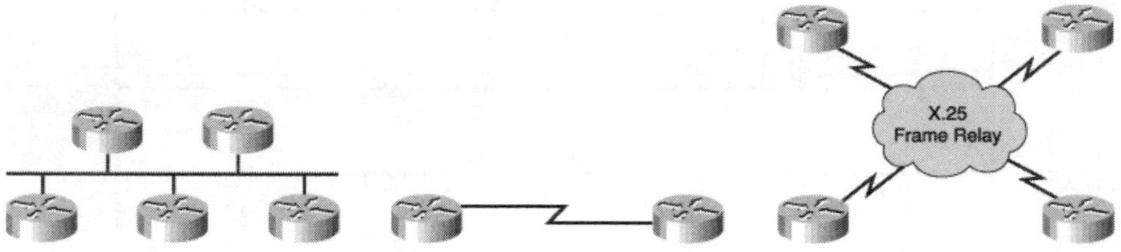

7   OSPF operations follow these steps:

Establish router _____.

Elect a _____ _____ and a _____ _____ _____.

_____ routes.

_____ appropriate routes to use.

_____ routing information

8. Because OSPF routing is dependent on the status of a link between two routers, neighbor routers must "_____" each other on the network before they can share information.

9. Another noteworthy point about OSPF is that it does not perform _____ and _____; these functions are performed at the IP layer.

10. Every OSPF packet shares a common ____-byte protocol header.

11. Fill in Figure 3-2, which shows the different parts of the OSPF header.

Figure 3-2   List the OSPF Header Fields

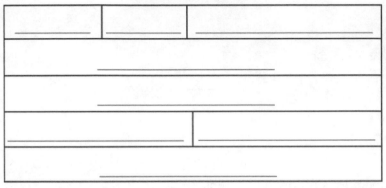

12. _____ packets are sent periodically out of each interface using IP multicast addresses.

13. The Hello process provides quicker detection of failed routers because Hellos are exchanged every ____ seconds. If a router is silent for ____ seconds, its neighbors believe it is down.

14. The _____ IP address on an active physical or loopback interface is the Router ID.

15. Routers from the same _____ each have the same link-state database information.

16. In a typical broadcast LAN environment such as Ethernet or Token Ring, the OSPF routers communicate with the DR using multicast address _____.

17. The following are used to determine which routers are elected as DR and BDR:

The router with the highest set _____ value is the ____.

The router with the second-highest set priority value is the _____.

The default value for OSPF interface priority is ___. In case of a tie, the router ___ is used as a tiebreaker.

The only time a DR or BDR changes is if one of them _____ _____.

18.   Fill in the circles pointing out the two DRs and one BDR in Figure 3-3.

Figure 3-3   *List the DRs and BDR*

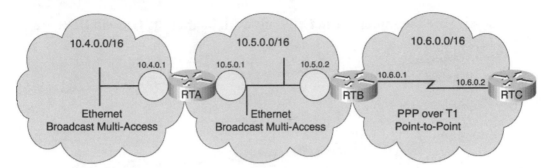

19.   After the DR and BDR have been elected, the routers are in the _____ state.

20.   The process used to discover the network routes is called the _____ process. It is performed to advance the routers to a _____ state of communication.

21.   The routers must be in the _____ state before they can route traffic.

22.   To calculate the lowest cost to a destination, link-state protocols such as OSPF use the _____ algorithm.

23.   Sometimes, a link goes up and down rapidly. This is called _____.

24.   The ___ _____ command was added to the Cisco IOS software to prevent routers from computing a new routing table until _____ seconds after a route change.

25.   When there is a change in a link state, the router uses a _____ process to notify the other routers in the network of the change.

26.   When a router notices a change in a link state, it _____ an LSU packet that includes the updated LSA entry to _____, the "all DR routers" (and BDR) address.

27.   Write the configuration entry to enable OSPF on a router:

_____

28.   _____ -_____ is a user-defined number that identifies multiple OSPF processes running in a single router.

CCNA Exam Review Questions

The following questions help you review for the CCNA exam. The answers appear in Appendix A, "Answers to CCNA Exam Review Questions."

1. What state are the routers in an OSPF network in after the DR and BDR are elected?

    A. Exstart
    B. Full
    C. Loading
    D. Exchange

2. What OSPF packet type establishes and maintains neighbor adjacencies?

    A. Link-state request
    B. Link-state acknowledgment
    C. Hello
    D. Database description packet

3. What is the default cost metric for OSPF based on?

    A. Delay
    B. Media bandwidth
    C. Efficiency
    D. Network traffic

4. What multicast address represents all OSPF routers?

    A. 224.0.0.6
    B. 224.0.0.1
    C. 224.0.0.4
    D. 224.0.0.5

5. What command can be used to change OSPF priority on an interface?

    A. **ip priority number ospf**
    B. **ip ospf priority number**
    C. **ospf priority number**
    D. **set priority ospf number**

6. What multicast address is used to send LSUs to all DR/BDR routers?

    A. 224.0.0.6

    B. 224.0.0.1

    C. 224.0.0.4

    D. 224.0.0.5

7. What is a common feature of NBMA networks?

    A. Support for only two routers

    B. Support for more than two routers

    C. No election of DRs

    D. Full support for broadcast and multicast packets

8. What command allows OSPF routers to exchange routing updates without multicasts?

    A. **ip ospf neighbor**

    B. **ospf neighbor**

    C. **neighbor**

    D. **ip neighbor**

9. What command displays the routes known to a router and how they were learned?

    A. **show ip protocol**

    B. **show ip route**

    C. **show ip ospf**

    D. **show ip ospf neighbor detail**

10. Which of the following are two basic types of dynamic routing?

    A. Static and default

    B. TCP and UDP exchange

    C. Distance vector and link-state

    D. None of the above

11. _____ routing protocols determine the direction and distance to any link in the internetwork; _____ routing protocols are also called shortest path first.

    A. Distance-vector, link-state

    B. Distance-vector, hybrid

    C. Link-state, distance-vector

    D. Dynamic, static

Chapter 4

EIGRP

Enhanced Interior Gateway Routing Protocol (EIGRP) is a Cisco-proprietary routing protocol based on Interior Gateway Routing Protocol (IGRP).

Unlike IGRP, which is a classful routing protocol, EIGRP supports classless interdomain routing (CIDR), allowing network designers to maximize address space by using CIDR and variable-length subnet mask (VLSM). Compared to IGRP, EIGRP boasts faster convergence times, improved scalability, and superior handling of routing loops.

Furthermore, EIGRP can replace Novell Routing Information Protocol (RIP) and AppleTalk Routing Table Maintenance Protocol (RTMP), serving both IPX and AppleTalk networks with powerful efficiency.

EIGRP is often described as a hybrid routing protocol offering the best of distance-vector and link-state algorithms. Technically, EIGRP is an advanced distance-vector routing protocol that relies on features commonly associated with link-state protocols. Some of the best features of OSPF, such as partial updates and neighbor discovery, are similarly used by EIGRP. However, EIGRP is easier to configure than OSPF.

EIGRP is an ideal choice for large multiprotocol networks built primarily on Cisco routers.

This chapter compares EIGRP and IGRP. It surveys the key concepts, technologies, and data structures of EIGRP. This conceptual overview is followed by a study of EIGRP convergence and basic operation using the EIGRP state-of-the-art routing algorithm called Diffusing Update Algorithm (DUAL).

Concept Questions

Demonstrate your knowledge of these concepts by answering the following questions in the space provided.

1. At what layer of the OSI model does path determination take place, and what is that layer's function?

   _____

   _____

   _____

2. How does a router determine on which interface to forward a data packet?

   _____

   _____

   _____

3.   What does the term *multiprotocol routing* mean?

_____

_____

_____

4.   What two basic router factors does a dynamic routing protocol depend on?

_____

_____

_____

5.   What does the term *convergence* mean in network implementation?

_____

_____

_____

Vocabulary Exercise

Define the following terms as completely as you can. Use the online curriculum or Chapter 4 of the *Cisco Networking Academy Program CCNA 3 and 4 Companion Guide*, Third Edition, for help.

DUAL

_____

_____

_____

feasible distance

_____

_____

_____

feasible successor

_____

_____

_____

holdtime

_____

_____

_____

neighbor address

_____

_____

_____

neighbor table

_____

_____

_____

queue count

_____

_____

_____

reported distance

_____

_____

_____

routing table

_____

_____

_____

RTP

_____

_____

_____

SRTT

_____

_____

_____

stuck in active

_____

_____

_____

successor

_____

_____

_____

topology table

_____

_____

_____

Focus Questions

1. There is only one minor difference in the algorithm that calculates the composite metric: The IGRP metric is _____ bits long, whereas the EIGRP metric is _____ bits long.

2. IGRP and EIGRP metrics are directly comparable; therefore, they can be used _____ after translation. EIGRP does, however, track the translated IGRP routes as _____ routes.

3. Automatic _____ between IGRP and EIGRP occurs only if the two protocols are configured with the same _____ _____ (_____) number. If they have different _____ numbers, they assume that they are part of different networks.

4. EIGRP is sometimes called a(n) _____ routing protocol.

    Some of the specific advantages of EIGRP include the following:

    _____ _____. EIGRP routers store every path they have learned to every destination in the network. Therefore, a router running EIGRP can quickly _____ on an alternative route after any topological change.

    Efficient use of _____ *during convergence.* EIGRP does not make periodic updates. Instead, it sends partial updates about a route when the path changes or when the metric for that route changes.
    When path information changes, the _____ algorithm sends an update about that link only, rather than about the entire table. In addition, the information is sent to only the routers that need it, in contrast to link-state protocol operation, which sends a change update to all routers in an area. In EIGRP, this is known as a _____, _____ _____.

    Minimal consumption of bandwidth when the network is stable. During normal, stable network operation, the only EIGRP packets exchanged between EIGRP nodes are _____ packets.

    Complete independence from routed protocols. EIGRP is designed to be completely independent of routed protocols. Support for routed protocols is via individual, protocol-specific _____.

    Multiple network-layer support. EIGRP supports _____ _____, _____, and _____ _____ through the use of protocol-dependent modules (PDMs).

5.   EIGRP supports _____ RIP and SAP updates. EIGRP sends out RIP and SAP updates only when _____ _____, and it sends out only the _____ information.

6.   EIGRP IPX networks have a diameter of ____ hops, instead of IPX RIP's ___-hop diameter.

EIGRP for Novell IPX provides optimal path selection. EIGRP for IPX uses _____ and _____ to determine the best route to a destination.

Redistribution of NetWare Link Services Protocol (NLSP) is _____ starting with Cisco IOS Release _____. NLSP is Novell's link state routing protocol for IPX-based networks.

7.   Fill in the steps in Figure 4-1 for EIGRP routers to converge.

Figure 4-1   Fill in the EIGRP Convergence Steps

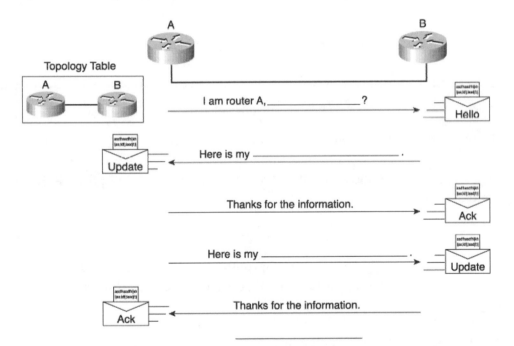

8. EIGRP includes many new technologies, each of which represents an improvement in operating efficiency, rapidity of convergence, or feature/functionality relative to IGRP and other routing protocols. These technologies fall into one of the following four categories:

Neighbor _____ and _____

_____ Transport Protocol

_____ finite-state machine

Protocol-specific _____

9. The basis for maintaining routing tables is a _____ communication between EIGRP routers. They use this process to

_____ learn of new routers that join their network

_____ routers that become either unreachable or inoperable

_____ routers that were previously unreachable

10. EIGRP was given a new protocol, the _____ _____ _____ (___), to provide reliable delivery of its own packets.

11. RTP is a transport-layer protocol that correlates to the functionality identified by Layer ___ of the OSI reference model.

12. RTP can support both reliable and unreliable delivery of _____.

13. The centerpiece of the new EIGRP technologies is _____, the EIGRP route-calculation engine.

The full name of the EIGRP engine is _____ _____-_____ _____.

14. A _____ _____ is a neighbor router that is the next hop in a least-cost path to any given destination. It is a path that is loop-free according to the _____ ____.

15. EIGRP uses many different tables, each dedicated to organizing and storing data pertinent to a specific facet of the network. They are

The _____ table

The _____ table

The _____ table

16. The single most important table in EIGRP is the _____ table. The _____ relationships tracked in this table are the basis of all the EIGRP routing update and convergence activity.

17. Additionally, a neighbor table is used to support reliable, _____ delivery of packets.

     _____ numbers are used to acknowledge specific packets that were delivered reliably.

     EIGRP records the number of the last message received from each _____.

18. The routing table contains the lowest-metric routes that _____ calculated for all known destinations. A _____ routing table is maintained for each _____ _____ that EIGRP is configured to support.

19. EIGRP uses its _____ table to store all the information it needs to calculate a set of distances and vectors to all known and reachable destinations. A _____ topology table is maintained for each protocol-dependent module being used by EIGRP. This table includes the following:

     The _____ of the slowest interface in the path to a destination effectively limits the route's performance and is used to calculate the route composite metric.

     _____ _____. This field contains the sum total of delay values in that route.

     The path's _____ is also recorded in the topology table.

     The path's _____ level is another IGRP metric that has been retained by EIGRP.

     The MTU field contains the size of the _____ maximum transmission unit (MTU) supported by the router interfaces in the path.

     The path's _____ _____ is the distance given by an adjacent neighbor to a specific destination.

     The _____ _____ is the lowest calculated metric to each destination.

     _____ _____ is the identification number of the router that originally advertised that route. This field is populated only for routes learned _____ from the EIGRP network.

20. To see the entire contents of the EIGRP topology table, execute this command:

     _____

21. Entries in a topology table can be in one of two states: _____ or _____.

     An _____ route is one currently being recomputed.

22. Hello packets are used to _____ and track other EIGRP routers in the network.

    Rediscovering a lost neighbor is known as _____ or _____.

23. _____ packets are used to acknowledge the receipt of any EIGRP packet that requires reliable delivery. _____ packets are always multicast, whereas _____ are always sent to a single, specific IP address. This is known as _____.

24. The _____ packet is used to convey routing information to known destinations.

    _____ packets are used whenever a router needs specific information from one or all of its neighbors. They are sent only when a destination becomes _____. A _____ packet is used to respond to a query.

25. The command to see the neighbor table is

    _____

CCNA Exam Review Questions

The following questions help you review for the CCNA exam. The answers appear in Appendix A, "Answers to CCNA Exam Review Questions."

1. How do you configure automatic redistribution between IGRP and EIGRP?

    A. Configure the two protocols with different AS numbers.

    B. Configure the two protocols with different DS numbers.

    C. Configure the two protocols with the same AS numbers.

    D. Configure the two protocols with the same DS numbers.

2. Which protocol combines the advantages of link-state and distance-vector routing protocols?

    A. RIP

    B. OSPF

    C. IGRP

    D. EIGRP

3. Which algorithm is used to achieve rapid convergence?

    A. Dijkstra's algorithm

    B. Diffusing Update Algorithm

    C. Convergence algorithm

    D. Dual convergence algorithm

4. Which protocol does EIGRP support through the use of protocol-dependent modules (PDMs)?

    A. IS-IS

    B. SNMP

    C. Novell NetWare

    D. DHCP

5. Which table includes route entries for all destinations that the router has learned and is maintained for each configured routing protocol?

    A. Topology table

    B. Routing table

    C. Neighbor table

    D. Successor table

6.   Which of the following establishes adjacencies in EIGRP?

   A.   DUAL finite-state machine

   B.   Hello packets

   C.   Topology table

   D.   Reliable transport protocol

7.   Which of the following guarantees ordered delivery of EIGRP packets to all neighbors?

   A.   DUAL finite-state machine

   B.   Hello packets

   C.   Topology table

   D.   Reliable transport protocol

8.   What does DUAL do after it tracks all routes, compares them, and guarantees that they are loop-free?

   A.   Inserts lowest-cost paths into the routing table

   B.   Determines the optimal path and advertises it to the neighbor routers using hello packets

   C.   Supports other routed protocols through PDMs

   D.   Sends a unicast query to the neighboring routers

9.   How does EIGRP prevent routing loops from occurring with external routes?

   A.   By rejecting external routes tagged with a router ID identical to their own

   B.   By storing the identities of neighbors that are feasible successors

   C.   By rejecting all neighboring routers that have an advertised composite metric that is less than a router's best current metric

   D.   By storing all neighboring routes that have loops identified in a special table

10.   On higher-bandwidth connections, such as point-to-point serial links or multipoint circuits, how long is the hello interval used by EIGRP?

   A.   5 seconds

   B.   10 seconds

   C.   60 seconds

   D.   120 seconds

Chapter 5

Switching Concepts

One of the most critical steps of ensuring a fast and stable network is the network's design. If a network is not designed properly, many unforeseen problems can arise, and network growth can be jeopardized. The trend is toward increasingly complex environments involving multiple media, multiple protocols, and connections to networks outside a single organization's control. Design is an in-depth process that includes the following:

- Gathering user requirements and expectations
- Determining data traffic patterns, now and in the future, based on growth and server placement
- Defining all the Layer 1, 2, and 3 devices, along with LAN and WAN topology
- Document the physical and logical network implementation

This chapter discusses problems in a local-area network (LAN) and possible solutions that can improve LAN performance. You learn about LAN congestion, its effect on network performance, and the advantages of LAN segmentation in a network. In addition, you learn about the advantages and disadvantages of using bridges, switches, and routers for LAN segmentation and the effects of switching, bridging, and routing on network throughput.

Concept Questions

Demonstrate your knowledge of these concepts by answering the following questions in the space provided.

1. The combination of more powerful computers/workstations and network-intensive applications has created a need for bandwidth that is much greater than the 10 Mbps available on shared Ethernet/802.3 LANs. What technology offers a solution to this bandwidth problem?

   _____

   _____

   _____

2. As more people use a network to share large files, access file servers, and connect to the Internet, network congestion occurs. What is network congestion, and what effect does it have on the network?

   _____

   _____

   _____

3. A network can be divided into smaller units called *segments*. Each segment is considered its own collision domain. Does this reduce network congestion? Explain.

_____

_____

_____

4. A LAN that uses a Switched Ethernet topology creates a network that behaves as if it has only two nodes—the sending node and the receiving node. Why is this so?

_____

_____

_____

5. Switches achieve high-speed transfer by reading the packet's destination Layer 2 MAC address, much the way a bridge does. This leads to a high rate of speed for packet forwarding. How does a switch differ from a bridge?

_____

_____

_____

6. Ethernet switching increases a network's available bandwidth. Exactly how does this occur? What is Gigabit Ethernet?

_____

_____

_____

7. Symmetric switching is one way of characterizing a LAN switch according to the bandwidth allocated to each port on the switch. Are there other ways of characterizing a LAN switch?

_____

_____

_____

8. An asymmetric LAN switch provides switched connections between ports of unlike bandwidth, such as a combination of 10-Mbps and 100-Mbps ports. What are the differences between symmetric and asymmetric switching? Can you draw a schematic of each?

    _____

    _____

9. The main function of the Spanning Tree Protocol is to allow duplicate switched/bridged paths without suffering the latency effects of loops in the network. What does this mean to a network manager, and why is it important?

    _____

    _____

    _____

Vocabulary Exercise

Define the following terms as completely as you can. Use the online curriculum or Chapter 5 of the *Cisco Networking Academy Program CCNA 3 and 4 Companion Guide*, Third Edition, for help.

10BASE-T

_____

_____

_____

100BASE-FX

_____

_____

_____

100BASE-TX

_____
_____
_____

1000BASE-CX

_____
_____
_____

1000BASE-LX

_____
_____
_____

1000BASE-SX

_____
_____
_____

1000BASE-T

_____
_____
_____

acknowledgment

_____
_____
_____

adaptability

_____
_____
_____

addressing

_____
_____
_____

ARP

_____
_____
_____

availability

_____

_____

_____

backbone

_____

_____

_____

bandwidth

_____

_____

_____

broadcast

_____

_____

_____

broadcast domain

_____

_____

_____

cable plant

_____

_____

_____

catchment area

_____

_____

_____

coaxial cable

_____

_____

_____

collision detection

_____

_____

_____

collision domain

_____

_____

_____

congestion

_____

_____

_____

contention

_____

_____

_____

CSMA/CD

_____

_____

_____

cut-through

_____

_____

_____

design

_____

_____

_____

Enterprise servers

_____

_____

_____

Ethernet 802.3

_____

_____

_____

Ethernet switch

_____

_____

_____

extended star topology

_____

_____

_____

Fast Ethernet

_____

_____

_____

fast-forward switching

_____

_____

_____

firewall

_____

_____

_____

fragment-free switching

_____

_____

_____

full-duplex Ethernet

_____

_____

_____

functionality

_____

_____

_____

Gigabit Ethernet

_____

_____

_____

HCC

_____

_____

_____

scalability

_____
_____
_____

segment

_____
_____
_____

segmentation

_____
_____
_____

single-mode fiber-optic cable

_____
_____
_____

sliding window

_____
_____
_____

star topology

_____
_____
_____

subnet

_____
_____
_____

switching

_____
_____
_____

topology

_____
_____
_____

twisted-pair cable

_____

_____

_____

VCC

_____

_____

_____

vertical cabling

_____

_____

_____

VLAN

_____

_____

_____

WAN

_____

_____

_____

workgroup server

_____

_____

_____

Focus Questions

1. Distinguish between cut-through and store-and-forward switching. Also describe the fast-forward and fragment-free switching techniques.

    _____

    _____

    _____

    _____

    _____

    _____

    _____

    _____

    _____

    _____

    _____

    _____

2. Describe full- and half-duplex Ethernet operation.

    _____

    _____

    _____

    _____

    _____

3. Describe the advantages of LAN segmentation that uses switches.

    _____

    _____

    _____

4. What are the differences between repeaters, hubs, bridges, switches, and routers?

    _____

    _____

    _____

    _____

    _____

    _____

    _____

    _____

    _____

5.   What is a multiport repeater?

_____

_____

_____

6.   What is the difference between Shared Ethernet and Switched Ethernet?

_____

_____

_____

CCNA Exam Review Questions

The following questions help you review for the CCNA exam. The answers appear in Appendix A, "Answers to CCNA Exam Review Questions."

1. Which of the following broadcast methods does an Ethernet medium use to transmit data to and receive data from all nodes on the network?

    A. A packet

    B. A data frame

    C. A segment

    D. A byte at a time

2. What is the minimum time it takes Ethernet to transmit 1 byte?

    A. 100 ns

    B. 800 ns

    C. 51,200 ns

    D. 800 ms

3. Which of the following are characteristics of microsegmentation?

    A. Dedicated paths between sender and receiver hosts.

    B. Multiple traffic paths within the switch.

    C. All traffic is visible on the network segment at once.

    D. A and B.

4. LAN switches are considered to be which of the following?

    A. Multiport repeaters operating at Layer 1

    B. Multiport hubs operating at Layer 2

    C. Multiport routers operating at Layer 3

    D. Multiport bridges operating at Layer 2

5. Asymmetric switching is optimized for which of the following?

    A. Client/server network traffic in which the "fast" switch port is connected to the server

    B. An even distribution of network traffic

    C. Switches without memory buffering

    D. A and B

6. In _____ switching, the switch checks the destination address and immediately begins forwarding the frame, and in _____ switching, the switch receives the complete frame before forwarding it.

    A. Store-and-forward, symmetric

    B. Cut-through, store-and-forward

    C. Store-and-forward, cut-through

    D. Memory buffering, cut-through

7. Which of the following is/are likely to cause congestion?

    A. Internet access

    B. Central database access

    C. Video and image transmission

    D. All of the above

8. Which of the following is *not* a cause of excessive broadcasts?

    A. Too many client packets looking for services

    B. Too many server packets announcing services

    C. Too many routing table updates

    D. Too many network segments

9. A primary data link layer design goal is the selection of _____ devices, such as bridges or LAN switches, used to connect _____ media to form LAN segments.

    A. Layer 3, Layer 2

    B. Layer 1, Layer 2

    C. Layer 2, Layer 1

    D. Layer 2, Layer 3

10. Which of the following specifications for 10BASE-T is wrong?

    A. Data rate is 10 Mbps

    B. Maximum length is 400 meters

    C. Signaling method is baseband

    D. Media is Category 5 UTP

11. Which of the following are benefits of implementing Layer 3 devices in your LAN?

    A. It allows segmentation of the LAN into unique physical and logical networks.

    B. It filters data-link broadcasts and multicasts and allows for WAN connectivity.

    C. It provides logical structure to the network.

    D. All of the above

Chapter 6

Switches

A switch is a Layer 2 network device that acts as the concentration point to connect workstations, servers, routers, hubs, and other switches.

A hub is an earlier type of concentration device that, like a switch, provides multiple ports. Hubs are inferior to switches because all devices connected to a hub reside in the same bandwidth domain, and collisions occur. Also, hubs operate only in half-duplex mode, which means that they can either send or receive data at any given time.

Switches are multiport bridges and are the standard technology for today's Ethernet local-area networks (LANs) that use a star topology. A switch provides a dedicated point-to-point virtual circuit between two connected networking devices, so no collisions occur. Switches can operate in full-duplex mode, which means that they can send and receive data simultaneously. The ability to understand and configure switches is essential for network support.

LANs span a single room, building, or set of buildings that are close together. A set of buildings that are on a site and that belong to a single organization are called a campus. The design of larger LANs is assisted by an approach that identifies the following:

- An access layer that connects end users to the LAN

- A distribution layer that provides policy-based connectivity between end-user LANs

- A core layer that provides the fastest connection between the distribution points

As the scale of a LAN increases to the size of a campus, there is a need for a variety of LAN switches. Each layer requires switches that are best suited for the tasks of each specific layer. The features, functions, and technical specifications of each switch vary depending on which layer they are designed for. Choosing the switches best suited for each layer ensures the best network performance for LAN users.

Understanding the role of each layer and the switches used in those layers is important for an effective switched LAN design.

Concept Questions

Demonstrate your knowledge of these concepts by answering the following questions in the space provided.

1. What is the purpose of using the **enable** command on a switch, and what features does this provide for an administrator?

_____

_____

2.   What are some benefits of using the three-layer Hierarchical Design Model?

_____

_____

_____

Vocabulary Exercise

Define the following terms as completely as you can. Use the online curriculum or Chapter 6 of the *Cisco Networking Academy Program CCNA 3 and 4 Companion Guide* for help.

acknowledgment

_____

_____

_____

attenuation

_____

_____

_____

backbone

_____

_____

_____

bandwidth

_____

_____

_____

bit

_____

_____

_____

BPDU

_____

_____

_____

bridge

_____

_____

_____

bridging

_____

_____

_____

broadcast

_____

_____

_____

byte

_____

_____

_____

client/server application

_____

_____

_____

collision

_____

_____

_____

collision domain

_____

_____

_____

congestion

_____

_____

_____

core layer

_____

_____

_____

CSMA/CD

_____

_____

_____

cut-through

_____

_____

_____

data link layer

_____

_____

_____

distribution layer

_____

_____

_____

fast-forward switching

_____

_____

_____

flooding

_____
_____
_____
_____

fragment-free switching

_____
_____
_____
_____

full-duplex Ethernet

_____
_____
_____
_____

half-duplex Ethernet

_____
_____
_____
_____

hub

_____
_____
_____

interface

_____
_____
_____

latency

_____
_____
_____

memory buffer

_____
_____
_____

microsegmentation

_____
_____
_____

network layer

_____
_____
_____

NIC

_____
_____
_____

node

_____
_____
_____

physical layer

_____
_____
_____

port

_____
_____
_____

propagation delay

_____

_____

_____

queue

_____

_____

_____

repeater

_____

_____

_____

segmentation

_____

_____

_____

switch

_____

_____

_____

switching

_____

_____

_____

Focus Questions

1. Which of the following broadcast methods does an Ethernet medium use to transmit and receive data to all nodes on the network?

   A. A packet

   B. A data frame

   C. A segment

   D. A byte at a time

2.   What is the minimum time it takes Ethernet to transmit 1 byte?

    A.   100 ns

    B.   800 ns

    C.   51,200 ns

    D.   800 microseconds

3.   Characteristics of microsegmentation include which of the following?

    A.   Dedicated paths between sender and receiver hosts

    B.   Multiple traffic paths within the switch

    C.   All traffic visible on network segment at once

    D.   A and B

4.   LAN switches are considered to be which of the following?

    A.   Multiport repeaters operating at Layer 1

    B.   Multiport hubs operating at Layer 2

    C.   Multiport routers operating at Layer 3

    D.   Multiport bridges operating at Layer 2

5.   Asymmetric switching is optimized for which of the following?

    A.   Client/server network traffic where the "fast" switch port is connected to the server

    B.   An even distribution of network traffic

    C.   Switches without memory buffering

    D.   A and B

6.   In _____ switching, the switch checks the destination address and immediately begins forwarding the frame, and in _____ switching, the switch receives the complete frame before forwarding it.

    A.   Store-and-forward; symmetric

    B.   Cut-through; store-and-forward

    C.   Store-and-forward; cut-through

    D.   Memory buffering; cut-through

7. The Spanning Tree Protocol allows which of the following?

    A. Routers to communicate link states

    B. Switches to communicate hop counts

    C. Bridges to communicate Layer 3 information

    D. Redundant network paths without suffering the effects of loops in the network

8. What is each segment considered to be in a network segmented by switches?

    A. Network

    B. Campus network

    C. Collision domain

    D. WAN

9. Which of the following is true of a full-duplex Ethernct switch?

    A. Collisions are virtually eliminated.

    B. Two cable pairs and a switched connection between each node are used.

    C. Connections between nodes are considered point-to-point.

    D. All of the above

10. Congestion causes which of the following?

    A. Lower reliability and low traffic

    B. A high rate of collisions

    C. Network unpredictability and high error rates

    D. Lower response times, longer file transfers, and network delays

11. Host A transmits to Host B. The communication is such that Host A stops sending information content packets and then Host B begins sending packets. Similarly, Host B stops when Host A starts transmitting again. The transmission type is which of the following?

    A. Full-duplex

    B. Half-duplex

    C. Simplex

    D. None of the above

12. Which of the following statements concerning packet forwarding in a LAN is *not* true?

A. The store-and-forward packet-switching technique is the one in which frames are completely processed before being forwarded to the appropriate port.

B. Store-and-forward packet switching is slower than cut-through packet switching.

C. Cut-through packet switching is also known as on-the-fly packet switching.

D. Buffering is required in cut-through packet switching if the network connection or link is slow.

13. Which of the following is true of a LAN switch?

A. It repairs network fragments called microsegments.

B. It is a very high-speed multiport bridge.

C. Lower bandwidth makes up for higher latency.

D. It requires new network interface cards on attached hosts.

14. How many collision domains are created by a 16-port LAN switch?

A. One

B. Two

C. Fourteen

D. Sixteen

15. If you create a virtual circuit with LAN switching, what is the result on that segment?

A. Increased collisions

B. Decreased available bandwidth

C. Increased broadcasts

D. Increased available bandwidth

16. How do switches learn the addresses of devices that are attached to their ports?

A. Switches get the tables from a router.

B. Switches read the source address of a packet entering through a port.

C. Switches exchange address tables with other switches.

D. Switches cannot build address tables.

17.   What is the purpose of symmetric switching?

A.   To provide switch connections on ports with the same bandwidths.

B.   To make sure the network tables are symmetrical.

C.   To provide switched connections on ports with different bandwidths.

D.   Switches provide only asymmetric switching.

4.   Define and describe how a switch handles broadcast domains, and describe how the use of routers reduces network traffic by reducing the size of a broadcast domain.

_____

_____

_____

_____

_____

_____

Vocabulary Exercise

Define the following terms as completely as you can. Use the online curriculum or Chapter 7 of the *Cisco Networking Academy Program CCNA 3 and 4 Companion Guide* for help.

asymmetric switching

_____

_____

_____

broadcast domain

_____

_____

_____

CAM

_____

_____

_____

collision domain

_____

_____

_____

cut-through switching

_____

_____

_____

fast-forward switching

_____
_____
_____

fragment-free switching

_____
_____
_____

memory buffering

_____
_____
_____

microsegment

_____
_____
_____

store-and-forward switching

_____
_____
_____

symmetric switching

_____
_____
_____

CCNA Exam Review Questions

The following questions help you review for the CCNA exam. The answers appear in Appendix A, "Answers to CCNA Exam Review Questions."

1. Which of the following are characteristics of microsegmentation?

   A. Dedicated paths between sender and receiver hosts

   B. Multiple traffic paths within the switch

   C. Increased collision domains

   D. All of the above

2. How are LAN switches characterized?

   A. Multiport repeaters operating at Layer 1

   B. Multiport hubs operating at Layer 2

   C. Multiport routers operating at Layer 3

   D. Multiport bridges operating at Layer 2

3. Asymmetric switching is optimized for which of the following?

   A. Client-server network traffic where the "fast" switch port is connected

   B. An even distribution of network traffic

   C. Switches without memory buffering

   D. Load balancing between links

4. In _____ switching, the switch checks the destination address and immediately begins forwarding the frame while in _____ switching the switch receives the complete frame before forwarding it.

   A. Store-and-forward;symmetric

   B. Cut-through; store-and-forward

   C. Store-and-forward; cut-through

   D. Memory buffering;cut-through

5. Fragment-free and fast-forward switching are two forms of _____ switching.

   A. Store-and-forward

   B. Memory-buffering

   C. Cut-through

   D. Symmetric

6. When connecting a workstation to a switch, what kind of cable do you use?

    A. Straight-through

    B. Crossover

    C. Null-modem

    D. Standard phone line

7. Which communication method is characterized by one host sending and one host receiving?

    A. Broadcast

    B. Unicast

    C. Multicast

    D. None of the above

8. Which of the following is true of accessing a switch by means of an Ethernet port?

    A. The console port must be configured first.

    B. A crossover cable connects the workstation to the switch port.

    C. The switch can be managed only through the console port.

    D. The switch must be configured with an IP address.

    E. None of the above

9. Which type of cable is used when connecting two switches?

    A. Straight-through

    B. Crossover

    C. Null-modem

    D. Standard phone line

    E. Rollover

    F. Console

10. Which of the following is true of **set** command-based switches?

    A. Configuration changes are made in global configuration mode.

    B. The **copy run start** command is used to save the configuration to NVRAM.

    C. The **clear config all** command resets the switch to the factory default configuration.

    D. The privileged mode prompt is Switch#.

11. What are two major classifications of Cisco Catalyst switches?

    A.   Cisco IOS software command-based and **set** command-based

    B.   **set** command-based and menu-driven

    C.   Cisco IOS software command-based and menu-driven

    D.   CLI-based and Cisco IOS software command-based

12. Unlike a router, a switch has only a single IP address. On which interface is this address defined?

    A.   Interface Ethernet 0 on a **set** command-based switch

    B.   Interface sc0 on an IOS command-bascd switch

    C.   Interface VLAN1 on a **set** command-based switch

    D.   Interface VLAN1 on a Cisco IOS software command-based switch

13. Which of the following best describes the effect of the command **set port speed 10/1 auto**?

    A.   Both the speed and duplex mode of the specified port are automatically negotiated.

    B.   The speed of the first port on module 10 is automatically negotiated.

    C.   Ports operating at 10 Mbps automatically negotiate their duplex mode.

    D.   Ports can negotiate a speed up to 10 times their base rate.

14. What command is used to view the active configuration of a **set** command-based switch?

    A.   **show config**

    B.   **show running-config**

    C.   **show active-config**

    D.   **show current-config**

Chapter 8

Spanning Tree Protocol

This chapter describes redundant topologies and how important they are for maintaining networks. In addition, this chapter describes the functionality of both the Spanning Tree Protocol (STP) and Rapid Spanning Tree Protocol (RSTP).

Having redundancy in a network is important. Redundancy allows networks to be fault-tolerant. Redundant topologies protect against network downtime due to the failure of a single link, port, or networking device. Redundant topologies based on switches and bridges are susceptible to broadcast storms, multiple-frame transmissions, and media access control database instability.

The Spanning Tree Protocol is a Layer 2 link-management protocol used to maintain a loop free network. STP was developed by the Digital Equipment Corporation (DEC). The DEC spanning-tree algorithm was subsequently revised by the IEEE 802 committee and published in the IEEE 802.1d specification. The DEC and the IEEE 802.1d algorithm are not the same, nor are they compatible. The Cisco switches, such as the Catalyst 1900 and the 2950, use the IEEE 802.1d STP.

The Spanning Tree Protocol defined in the IEEE 802.1d standard has been found to be too slow in converging on a new topology for today's networks. A new standard, IEEE 802.1w, the Rapid Spanning Tree Protocol, has been defined to overcome known limitations.

Concept Questions

Demonstrate your knowledge of these concepts by answering the following questions in the space provided.

1. Describe the goals of redundant topologies.

2. Define the role that Spanning Tree Protocol plays in switched networks.

3.   Describe the stages of selecting a root bridge.

_____
_____
_____
_____
_____
_____

4.   Describe Rapid Spanning Tree Protocol.

_____
_____
_____
_____
_____
_____

Vocabulary Exercise

Define the following terms as completely as you can. Use the online curriculum or Chapter 8 of the *Cisco Networking Academy Program CCNA 3 and 4 Companion Guide* for help.

ARP

_____
_____
_____

BPDU

_____
_____
_____

broadcast domain

_____
_____
_____

collision domain

_____
_____
_____

cost

_____
_____
_____

MAC

_____
_____
_____

metric

_____
_____
_____

packet

_____
_____
_____

path determination

_____
_____
_____

reference point

_____
_____
_____

source address

_____
_____
_____

spanning tree

_____
_____
_____

Spanning Tree Protocol

_____

_____

_____

spanning-tree algorithm

_____

_____

_____

TTL

_____

_____

_____

Focus Questions

1. The Spanning Tree Protocol (_____) is a _____ prevention protocol. It is a technology that allows _____ to communicate with each other to discover _____ _____ in the network. The protocol then specifies an _____ that bridges can use to create a loop-free logical topology.

2. Usually loops in networks are the result of a deliberate attempt to provide _____.

3. Loops can be disastrous in a bridged network for two primary reasons: _____- _____ and bridge-table _____.

4. Bridging loops are much more/less dangerous than routing loops because Ethernet (unlike IP) does not have a _____ field.

5. A _____-_____ (____) is a single 8-byte field that is composed of two subfields. The low-order subfield consists of a 6-byte MAC address assigned to the switch. The high-order BID subfield is called the _____-_____. This field is a 2-byte (16-bit) value. This field can have values that range from _____ to _____. The default bridge priority is the midpoint value, _____.

6. The key point to remember concerning STP cost values is that _____ costs are better.

7.   In the following table, list the new STP path cost values for the bandwidth numbers.

Bandwidth	STP Cost
4 Mbps	
10 Mbps	
16 Mbps	
45 Mbps	
100 Mbps	
155 Mbps	
622 Mbps	
1 Gbps	
10 Gbps	

8.   Bridges pass spanning-tree information between themselves using special frames known as _____ _____ _____ _____ (_____s).

9.   A bridge uses the four-step decision sequence to save a copy of the _____ BPDU seen on every port.

10. When a bridge first becomes active, all its ports send BPDUs every _____ seconds. However, if a port hears a BPDU from another bridge that is _____ _____ than the BPDU it has been sending, the local port stops sending BPDUs.

11. The initial convergence of STP switches can be broken into three simple steps:

     1) _____ _____ _____ _____
     2) _____ _____ _____
     3) _____ _____ _____ _____

12. BPDUs are _____-to-_____ traffic; they do not carry _____-_____ traffic.

13. STP costs are incremented as BPDUs are _____ on a port, not as they are _____ _____ a port.

14.   Fill in the path costs in the balloons in Figure 8-1.

Figure 8-1   List the Path Costs

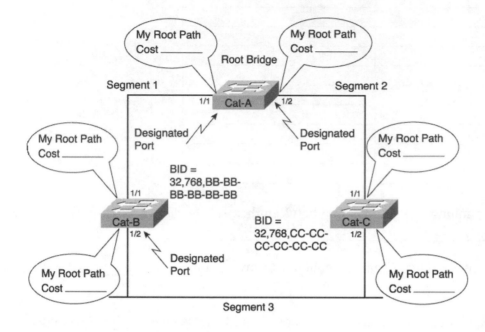

15.   Each segment in a bridged network has _____ designated port. This port functions as the _____ _____ port that both sends and receives _____ to and from that segment and the root bridge.

16.   The idea behind designated ports is that if only one port handles traffic for each link, all the _____ have been broken. The bridge containing the designated port for a given segment is referred to as the _____ _____ for that segment.

17.   Describe the STP states listed in the following table.

State	Purpose
Forwarding	
Learning	
Listening	

Blocking	
Disabled	

18. In Figure 8-2, fill in the blank boxes with the switch's STP st.

Figure 8-2   Identify the Switch STP State

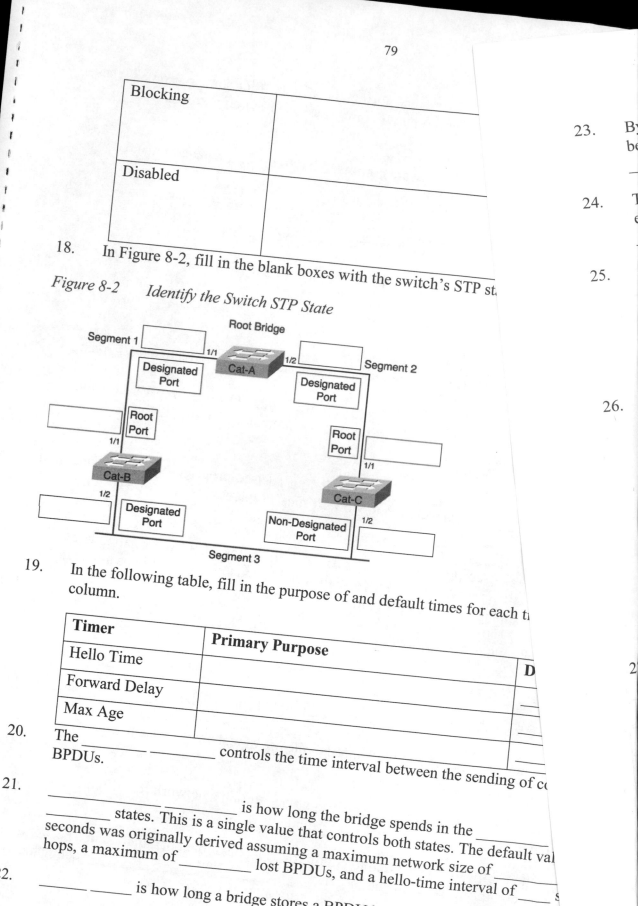

19. In the following table, fill in the purpose of and default times for each ti
column.

Timer	Primary Purpose	D
Hello Time		
Forward Delay		
Max Age		

20. The _____ _____ controls the time interval between the sending of c
BPDUs.

21. _____ _____ _____ is how long the bridge spends in the _____
_____ states. This is a single value that controls both states. The default val
seconds was originally derived assuming a maximum network size of _____
hops, a maximum of _____ lost BPDUs, and a hello-time interval of ____ s

22. _____ _____ is how long a bridge stores a BPDU before discarding it.

23. B
be

24. T
e

25.

26.

default, STP is _____ for every port on the switch. If for some reason STP has
en disabled, you can reenable it on a **set** command-based switch with the _____
_____ _____ command.

o enable STP on a Cisco IOS software command-based system, what command do you
nter in global configuration mode?

_____ _____ _____ output can be broken into four sections:

_____ statistics for the current switch/bridge (lines 2-4)

_____-_____ statistics (lines 5-9)

_____-_____ statistics (lines 10-12)

_____ statistics (lines 13-16)

The following describes some of the major methods of reconciling STP and VLANs:

_____ _____ _____ (_____) is the IEEE 802.1Q solution to VLANs and
spanning tree. CST defines a single instance of spanning tree for all VLANs. BPDU
information runs on VLAN 1.

_____ _____ _____ (_____) is a Cisco-proprietary implementation. It
requires _____ encapsulation to work. It runs a separate instance of STP for every
VLAN.

_____ is a Cisco-proprietary implementation that allows CST information to be
passed correctly into PVST. A solution to the scaling and stability problems associated
with large spanning-tree networks is to create separate instances of PVST.

Scaling STP involves the following tasks:

7.

Providing for an optimal topology through the proper _____ of the root bridge

Providing for efficient workstation access through the use of the _____ command

Load balancing on redundant links through the use of technologies such as _____
and _____ _____

Improving the convergence time of spanning tree during a network reconfiguration
through the use of _____ and _____.

28. The switch software can be used to configure STP operational parameters in a network.
     On a **set** command-based switch, use the _____ _____ _____ command to
     set the primary root for specific VLANs or for all the switch's VLANs.

29. To configure the STP root switch on a Cisco IOS command-based switch, enter the following command in _____ configuration mode:

_____

30. Use the _____ _____ command in privileged mode on a **set** command-based switch to verify the operation and state of each port and VLAN.

Use _____ _____ in an IOS switch.

31. After the root bridge has been elected, all switches determine the best loop-free path to the root. STP uses several different costs in determining the best path to the root bridge: _____ _____, _____ _____, and _____ _____.

32. Another mechanism for redundant links in a spanning-tree environment is _____ _____ technology. This technology allows spanning tree to treat _____ links as one _____ link.
In addition to providing high bandwidth, it also provides _____ _____ and _____.

33. Fast EtherChannel and Gigabit EtherChannel use a load distribution _____ based on the destination _____ address.

34. A _____ is a group of links managed by the Fast EtherChannel process. Fast EtherChannel technology provides statistical _____ _____ of connections over multiple links in a bundle.

35. _____-_____ time is the time it takes for the new address to be relearned. Assuming that one packet sent by the source results in an instant response, failover takes place as quickly as _____ _____.

36. The _____ _____ _____ (_____) adds additional features to Fast EtherChannel technology. It aids in the automatic creation of Fast EtherChannel links.

37. When using Fast EtherChannel, configure all ports in a channel to operate at the same _____ and _____ _____ (full or half duplex).

38. _____ is a feature that is designed primarily to optimize switch ports that are connected to end-station devices.
By using PortFast, these devices can be granted instant access to the Layer 2 network without going through the spanning tree _____ and _____ stages.

39. _____ allows a blocked port on a switch to almost immediately begin forwarding when the switch detects the failure of the forwarding link.
_____ must have direct knowledge of the link failure to move a blocked port into a forwarding state.

CCNA Exam Review Questions

The following questions help you review for the CCNA exam. The answers appear in Appendix A, "Answers to CCNA Exam Review Questions."

1. The goal of redundant topologies is to eliminate network outages caused by how many points of failure?

    A. One

    B. Two

    C. Three

    D. Four

2. What is the purpose of the Spanning Tree Protocol?

    A. To maintain single-loop paths

    B. To maintain a loop-free network

    C. To maintain a multiloop network

    D. To maintain a reduced-loop network

3. When the network topology changes, what happens?

    A. You must initiate a spanning-tree recalculation.

    B. You must reconfigure the top node of the spanning tree.

    C. You must reconfigure all devices participating in the spanning tree.

    D. The Spanning Tree Protocol reconfigures switch or bridge ports automatically.

4. On the root bridge, all ports are what?

    A. Root ports

    B. Blocked ports

    C. Designated ports

    D. Nondesignated ports

5. How does the Spanning Tree Protocol select the root port on a nonroot bridge?

    A. The root port is the highest-cost path from the nonroot bridge to the root bridge.

    B. The root port is the lowest-cost path from the nonroot bridge to the root bridge.

    C. The root port is the lowest-cost path from the nonroot bridge to the backup root bridge.

    D. The root port is the highest-cost path from the nonroot bridge to the backup root bridge.

6.   Which bridge does the Spanning Tree Protocol select as the root bridge?

    A.   The one with the lowest priority

    B.   The one with the lowest bridge ID

    C.   The one with the highest bridge ID

    D.   The one with the highest MAC address

7.   What comprises the Spanning Tree Protocol bridge ID?

    A.   Bridge priority and bridge IP address

    B.   Bridge priority and bridge MAC address

    C.   Bridge MAC address and bridge IP address

    D.   Bridge MAC address and Ethernet port number

8.   In what state can a port populate its MAC address table but not forward user frames?

    A.   Learning state

    B.   Blocking state

    C.   Listening state

    D.   Forwarding state

9.   In the revised IEEE specification, what is the cost of a 100-Mbps link?

    A.   4

    B.   10

    C.   19

    D.   100

10.   What is the definition of convergence for the Spanning Tree Protocol?

    A.   All the ports have transitioned to the blocking state.

    B.   All the ports have transitioned to the forwarding state.

    C.   All the ports have transitioned to either the forwarding or listening state.

    D.   All the ports have transitioned to either the forwarding or blocking state.

11.   What is the default max_age for the Spanning Tree Protocol?

    A.   2 seconds

    B.   15 seconds

    C.   20 seconds

    D.   30 seconds

12. What Rapid Spanning Tree Protocol state is equivalent to the Spanning Tree Protocol blocking state?

   A. Blocking

   B. Dropping

   C. Discarding

   D. Forwarding

13. What port role specifies a forwarding port elected for every switched LAN segment when using the Rapid Spanning Tree Protocol?

   A. Root

   B. Backup

   C. Alternate

   D. Designated

14. How does the STP provide a loop-free network?

   A. By placing all ports in the blocking state

   B. By placing all bridges in the blocking state

   C. By placing some ports in the blocking state

   D. By placing all bridges in the forwarding state

Chapter 9

VLANs

This chapter introduces virtual LANs (VLANs) and switched internetworking, compares traditional shared LAN configurations with switched LAN configurations, and discusses the benefits of using a switched VLAN architecture. When you finish the Chapter 9 online material and the print material in the *Cisco Networking Academy Program CCNA 3 and 4 Companion Guide,* you should completely understand the following concepts.

Concept Questions

Demonstrate your knowledge of these concepts by answering the following questions in the space provided.

1. An Ethernet switch is designed to segment a LAN into individual collision domains. Explain how an Ethernet switch works.

2. VLAN technology is a cost-effective and efficient way to group network users into virtual workgroups, regardless of their physical location on the network. Explain why.

3. VLANs work at Layer 2 and Layer 3 of the OSI reference model. Explain why this is so.

4. Important to any VLAN architecture is the capability to transport VLAN information between interconnected switches and routers that reside on the corporate backbone. Why is this so important?

5. The problems associated with shared LANs and switches are causing traditional LAN configurations to be replaced with switched VLAN networking configurations. Why do VLAN configurations solve the shared LAN and switches problem?

    _____

    _____

    _____

    _____

6. The most common approaches for logically grouping users into distinct VLANs are frame filtering, tagging, and frame identification. Explain how these approaches are used in VLANs.

    _____

    _____

    _____

    _____

    _____

    _____

7. VLANs reduce administrative costs related to solving problems associated with moves, additions, and changes. How do VLANs do this?

    _____

    _____

    _____

    _____

8. VLANs provide controlled broadcast activity. What is this?

    _____

    _____

    _____

9. VLANs provide workgroup and network security. How is this accomplished?

    _____

    _____

    _____

    _____

    _____

10.   Why are VLANs less expensive to implement and what would be the alternative ?

_____
_____
_____
_____

Vocabulary Exercise

Define the following terms as completely as you can. Use the online curriculum or Chapter 9 from the *Cisco Networking Academy Program CCNA 3 and 4 Companion Guide* for help.

ACL

_____
_____
_____

broadcast

_____
_____
_____

broadcast domain

_____
_____
_____

broadcast storm

_____
_____
_____

collision domain

_____
_____
_____

dynamic VLAN

_____
_____
_____

firewall

_____
_____
_____

flat network

_____
_____
_____

frame

_____
_____
_____

hub

_____
_____
_____

MAC

_____
_____
_____

microsegmentation

_____
_____
_____

multicast

_____
_____
_____

port

_____
_____
_____

port-centric VLAN

_____

_____

_____

static VLAN

_____

_____

_____

VLAN

_____

_____

_____

Focus Questions

1. What network problems might be caused if many LAN users change their location in a building over the course of a year?

    _____

    _____

    _____

2. Describe the benefits of VLANs.

    _____

    _____

    _____

3. What is the effect of VLANs on LAN broadcasts?

    _____

    _____

    _____

4. What are the three main VLAN implementations?

    _____

    _____

    _____

5. What is the purpose of VLAN frame tagging?

    _____

    _____

    _____

6. You are discussing installing a network for a customer. Outline the presentation you would give to the customer, explaining VLANs and how you intend to put this technology to use in his or her application. Include a script of your opening and closing paragraph.

CCNA Exam Review Questions

The following questions help you review for the CCNA exam. The answers appear in Appendix A, "Answers to CCNA Exam Review Questions."

1. What does the phrase *microsegmentation with scalability* mean?

    A. The ability to enlarge networks without creating collision domains

    B. The ability to put a huge number hosts on one switch

    C. The ability to broadcast to more nodes at once

    D. All of the above

2. Switches, as the core element of VLANs, provide the intelligence to do which of the following?

    A. Group users, ports, or logical addresses into a VLAN

    B. Make filtering and forwarding decisions

    C. Communicate with other switches and routers

    D. All of the above

3. Each _____ segment connected to a _____ port can be assigned to only one VLAN.

    A. Switch, hub

    B. Hub, router

    C. Hub, switch

    D. LAN, hub

4. Which of the following is *not* an advantage of using static VLANs?

    A. They are secure.

    B. They are easy to configure.

    C. They are easy to monitor.

    D. They automatically configure ports when new stations are added.

5. Which of the following is *not* a criterion on which VLANs can be based?

    A. Port ID and MAC address

    B. Protocol

    C. Application

    D. All of the above are criteria on which VLANs can be based.

6.   Which of the following is *not* a beneficial effect of adding a VLAN?

   A.   Switches do not need to be configured.

   B.   Broadcasts can be controlled.

   C.   Confidential data can be protected.

   D.   Physical boundaries that prevent user groupings can be removed.

Chapter 10

VLAN Trunking Protocol

This chapter discusses the origins of trunking and its operation. It also covers how VLAN Trunking Protocol (VTP) can solve some of your problems when you manage and implement VLANs in a large LAN network environment. Inter-VLAN routing also is discussed. After you finish the Chapter 10 online material and the print material in the *Cisco Networking Academy Program CCNA 3 and 4 Companion Guide,* you should better understand the following concepts.

Concept Questions

Demonstrate your knowledge of these concepts by answering the following questions in the space provided.

1. VLAN Trunking Protocol (VTP) was created to solve potential operational problems in a VLAN switched environment. Explain the fundamentals of VTP.

2. The role of VTP is to maintain VLAN configuration consistency across the entire network. Explain its benefits.

3. VTP switches operate in one of three modes . Explain these modes.

4. VTP Version 2 supports features not supported in Version 1. What are they?

    _____

    _____

    _____

5. A switch's default behavior is to propagate broadcast and unknown packets across the network. This behavior causes a large amount of unnecessary traffic to cross the network. What is VTP pruning?

    _____

    _____

    _____

6. In switched networks, route processors enable communication between VLANs. What do route processors provide?

    _____

    _____

    _____

7. As the number of VLANs increases in a network, network administrators must determine whether they want to have an individual router interface for each VLAN. What are possible solutions?

    _____

    _____

    _____

Vocabulary Exercise

Define the following terms as completely as you can. Use the online curriculum or Chapter 10 of the *Cisco Networking Academy Program CCNA 3 and 4 Companion Guide* for help.

802.1Q

_____

_____

_____

default gateway

_____

_____

_____

default router

ISL

---

router processor

---

trunking

VLANs

Focus Questions

1.   What is trunking?

   ---

2.   What do trunking protocols allow?

   ---

3.   What is frame tagging?

_____
_____
_____

4.   What are the Fast Ethernet and Gigabit Ethernet trunking modes, and what do they mean?

_____
_____

_____
_____

_____
_____

_____
_____

5.   What are the benefits of VTP?

_____
_____
_____

CCNA Exam Review Questions

The following questions help you review for the CCNA exam. The answers appear in Appendix A, "Answers to CCNA Exam Review Questions."

1. What is the primary advantage of using a trunk link?

   A. It provides more bandwidth for each trunk.
   B. It reduces router and switch ports.
   C. It allows for a single VLAN on each physical port.
   D. It creates less overhead on the router.

2. What protocol is Cisco-proprietary and is designed to carry traffic from multiple VLANs?

   A. 802.11A
   B. 802.1Q
   C. VNET
   D. ISL

3. VTP messages are encapsulated in either Cisco-proprietary Inter-Switch Link (ISL) or what type of frame?

   A. IEEE 802.1D protocol frame
   B. IEEE 802.1R protocol frame
   C. 802.11D protocol frame
   D. 802.19 protocol frame

4. True or false: Two different versions of VTP can run in your management domain, VTP Version 1 and VTP Version 2. The two versions are interoperable.

   A. True
   B. False

5. A switch's default behavior is to propagate broadcasts and unknown _____ across the network.

   A. Frames
   B. Packets
   C. Tags
   D. VLANs

6.   In switched networks, _____ is/are used to provide communication between VLANs.

   A.   Route processors
   B.   Modulators
   C.   VT
   D.   Subnets

Chapter 11

Scaling IP Addresses

IP is the connectivity protocol of choice. IP applications are being developed quickly, meaning that more hosts can potentially be connected to the Internet. In the early stages of the Internet, PCs, workstations, servers, and routers were the only devices attached to the Internet. IP addresses were statically assigned by an administrator.

Today, PDAs, laptops, desktops, mainframes, storage devices, routers, switches, video game consoles, and security cameras connect to the Internet. There is talk of even connecting household appliances. It should be clear that without scaling options, the Internet revolution would quickly reach its limits.

This chapter presents solutions to the IP scaling problem: NAT, DHCP, and RFC 1918.

Concept Questions

Demonstrate your knowledge of these concepts by answering the following questions in the space provided.

1. Describe why scaling IP addresses is necessary.

2. Describe NAT terminology and features.

3. Describe the difference between static NAT, dynamic NAT, and PAT.

4.   Describe the difference between BootP and DHCP.

_____
_____
_____
_____

Vocabulary Exercise

Define the following terms as completely as you can. Use the online curriculum or Chapter 11 of the *Cisco Networking Academy Program CCNA 3 and 4 Companion Guide* for help.

BootP

_____
_____
_____

Bootstrap

_____
_____
_____

DHCP

_____
_____
_____

inside global address

_____
_____
_____

inside local address

_____
_____
_____

NAT

_____
_____
_____

outside global address

_____
_____
_____

outside local address

_____
_____
_____

overloading

_____
_____
_____

CCNA Exam Review Questions

The following questions help you review for the CCNA exam. The answers appear in Appendix A, "Answers to CCNA Exam Review Questions."

1. Who or what assigns private addresses?

   A. The network administrator from RFC 1918

   B. American Registry for Internet Numbers (ARIN)

   C. Réseaux IP Européennes (RIPE)

   D. Any address can be a private address

2. Which of the following are valid RFC 1918 private addresses? (Choose all that apply.)

   A. 10.0.0.0/8

   B. 192.168.0.0/16

   C. 172.16.0.0/12

   D. All of the above

3. The BOX company maintains its own public web server, and it is about to implement NAT. Which type of NAT will be used for the web server?

   A. Dynamic

   B. Static

   C. PAT

   D. No NAT at all

4. Which type of NAT will be used for the CEO workstation in the BOX company?

   A. Dynamic

   B. Static

   C. PAT

   D. No NAT at all

5. Which of the following applications does Cisco IOS NAT support? (Choose all that apply.)

   A. ICMP

   B. DNS zone transfers

   C. BootP

   D. File Transfer Protocol (FTP) (including PORT and PASV)

6.   Which of the following traffic types does Cisco IOS NAT not support? (Choose all that apply.)

   A.   ICMP

   B.   DNS zone transfers

   C.   BootP

   D.   File Transfer Protocol (FTP) (including PORT and PASV)

7.   BootP supports _____, and DHCP supports _____.

   A.   Static mapping, dynamic mapping

   B.   PAT, NAT

   C.   RTP, PAT

   D.   NAT, DHCP

8.   What is the order of DHCP messages?

   A.   DHCPACK, DHCPOFFER, DHCPREQUEST, DHCPDISCOVER

   B.   DHCPREQUEST, DHCPACK, DHCPDISCOVER, DHCPOFFER

   C.   DHCPOFFER, DHCPDISCOVER, DHCPREQUEST, DHCPACK

   D.   DHCPDISCOVER, DHCPOFFER, DHCPREQUEST, DHCPACK

Chapter 12

WAN Technologies

As an enterprise grows beyond a single location, it becomes necessary to interconnect the local-area networks (LANs) in the various branches to form an enterprise wide-area network (WAN). This chapter examines some of the available options for these interconnections, the hardware needed to make them, and the terminology used in discussing them.

Concept Questions

Demonstrate your knowledge of these concepts by answering the following questions in the space provided.

1. What is a WAN?

   _____

   _____

   _____

   _____

2. Describe WAN encapsulation.

   _____

   _____

   _____

   _____

3. What is circuit switching?

   _____

   _____

   _____

4. What is packet switching?

   _____

   _____

   _____

5. What are some examples of circuit-switched connections?

   _____

   _____

6.   Describe some of the main features and concepts of ISDN, including the various types of interfaces that an ISDN connection can make.

_____

_____

_____

_____

7.   Describe some of the main features and concepts of Frame Relay connections.

_____

_____

_____

_____

8.   Describe some of the main features and concepts of ATM connections.

_____

_____

_____

_____

Vocabulary Exercise

Define the following terms as completely as you can. Use the online curriculum or Chapter 12 of the *Cisco Networking Academy Program CCNA 3 and 4 Companion Guide* for help.

ATM

_____

_____

_____

circuit switching

_____

_____

_____

CO

_____

_____

_____

CPE

_____

_____

_____

CSU

_____

_____

_____

DCE

_____

_____

_____

DSU

_____

_____

_____

DTE

_____

_____

_____

Frame Relay

_____

_____

_____

ISDN

_____

_____

_____

packet switching

_____
_____
_____

PVC

_____
_____
_____

SVC

_____
_____
_____

TDM

_____
_____
_____

CCNA Exam Review Questions

The following questions help you review for the CCNA exam. The answers appear in Appendix A, "Answers to CCNA Exam Review Questions."

1. Which of the following statements pertaining to ISDN is true?

    A. The ISDN BRI offers two B channels and one D channel.

    B. The D channel, operating at 16 Kbps, is meant to carry user data.

    C. The ISDN BRI offers 23 B channels and one D channel in North America.

    D. The total bit rate of the ISDN BRI is 2.533 Mbps.

2. Which of the following statements is *not* true of ATM technology?

    A. It can transfer voice, video, and data.

    B. ATM offers higher bandwidth than Frame Relay.

    C. It has a cell-based architecture rather than a frame-based architecture.

    D. ATM cells are always a fixed length of 35 bytes.

3. What is equipment on a subscriber's premises that connects to a service provider's central office called?

    A. DTE

    B. DCE

    C. CPE

    D. None of the above

4. Which of the following is *not* a circuit-switched connection?

    A. SONET

    B. Plain Old Telephone System (POTS)

    C. ISDN Basic Rate Interface (BRI)

    D. ISDN Primary Rate Interface (PRI)

5. Which of the following is *not* a packet-switched connection?

    A. Frame Relay

    B. X.25

    C. Asynchronous Transfer Mode (ATM)

    D. SONET

6.   ISDN BRI is composed of which of the following?

    A.   Two B channels and two D channels

    B.   Two B channels and one D channel

    C.   23 B channels and one D channel

    D.   30 B channels and one D channel

Chapter 13

PPP

You have studied wide-area network (WAN) technologies. Now it is important to understand that WAN connections are controlled by protocols that perform the same basic functions as Layer 2 LAN protocols, such as Ethernet. In a LAN environment, to move data between any two nodes or routers, a data path must be established, and flow control procedures must be in place to ensure delivery of data. This is also true in the WAN environment. These tasks are accomplished using WAN protocols.

In this chapter, you learn about the basic components, processes, and operations that define Point-to-Point Protocol (PPP) communication. In addition, this chapter discuss the use of Link Control Protocol (LCP) and Network Control Program (NCP) frames PPP. Finally, you learn how to configure and verify the configuration of PPP, along w PPP authentication, and you learn to use Password Authentication Protocol (PAP) and Challenge Handshake Authentication Protocol (CHAP).

Concept Questions

Demonstrate your knowledge of these concepts by answering the following questions the space provided.

1. Discuss the difference between LCP and NCP.

    _____

    _____

    _____

2. Configure the interface for PPP encapsulation.

3.	What changes in the router configuration must occur to implement PPP on the routers?

_____

_____

_____

4.	CHAP provides protection against playback attacks through the use of a variable
	challenge value. How and why does this work?

_____

_____

_____

Vocabulary Exercise

Define the following terms as completely as you can. Use the online curriculum or
Chapter 13 of the *Cisco Networking Academy Program CCNA 3 and 4 Companion Guide*
for help.

AppleTalk

_____

_____

_____

asynchronous circuits

_____

_____

_____

asynchronous physical medium

_____

_____

_____

authentication phase

_____

_____

_____

CHAP

---

encapsulation

HDLC

LCP

---

link establishment

---

link establishment phase

NCP

CCNA Exam Review Questions

The following questions help you review for the CCNA exam. The answers appear in Appendix A, "Answers to CCNA Exam Review Questions."

1. Which of the following is/are the network-layer protocol(s) supported by PPP? (Choose all that apply.)

    A.   Novell IPX

    B.   TCP/IP

    C.   AppleTalk

    D.   All of the above

2. In a PPP frame, what field identifies whether you have encapsulated IPX or TCP/IP?

    A.   Flag

    B.   Control

    C.   Protocol

    D.   FCS

3. When you're running PPP, LCP is responsible for which of the following?

    A.   Establishing, maintaining, and terminating the point-to-point connection

    B.   Maintaining several links

    C.   Router updates

    D.   Compression

4. What type of handshaking occurs when PAP is the selected PPP authentication protocol?

    A.   One-way

    B.   Two-way

    C.   Three-way

    D.   Four-way

5. What command on the router can you use to check the LCP and NCP states for PPP?

    A.   router> **show interfaces**

    B.   router(config)# **show interfaces**

    C.   router# **show interfaces**

    D.   router(config-if)# **show interfaces**

Chapter 14

ISDN and DDR

Many types of WAN technologies can be implemented to solve connectivity issues for users who need access to geographically distant locations. In this chapter, you learn about the services, standards, components, operation, and configuration of Integrated Services Digital Network (ISDN) communication. ISDN is designed to solve the problems of small offices or dial-in users who need more bandwidth than traditional telephone dial-in services can provide. ISDN also provides backup links.

Telephone companies developed ISDN with the intention of creating a totally digital network. ISDN was developed to use the existing telephone wiring system, and it works much like a telephone. When you want to make a data call with ISDN, the WAN link is brought up for the duration of the call, and it is taken down when the call is completed; it's similar to how you call a friend on the phone and hang up when you finish talking.

Concept Questions

Demonstrate your knowledge of these concepts by answering the following questions in the space provided.

1. What additional equipment do you need to establish an ISDN link for the WAN?

2. What are the most common uses for ISDN?

3. Which type of ISDN service will you use for your project, BRI or PRI? What are the differences between the two?

4. What configuration process is needed to implement an ISDN connection?

5.   What are the major advantages of an ISDN connection?

_____

_____

_____

6.   Briefly describe DDR.

_____

_____

_____

Vocabulary Exercise

Define the following terms as completely as you can. Use the online curriculum or Chapter 14 of the *Cisco Networking Academy Program CCNA 3 and 4 Companion Guide* for help.

2B+D

_____

_____

_____

B channel

_____

_____

_____

BRI

_____

_____

_____

CO

_____

_____

_____

CPE

_____

_____

_____

D channel

_____

_____

_____

DDR

_____

_____

_____

ISDN

_____

_____

_____

LAPB

_____

_____

_____

LAPD

_____

_____

_____

NT1

_____

_____

_____

NT2

_____

_____

_____

PBX

_____

_____

_____

PRI

_____

_____

_____

Q.931

_____

_____

_____

reference point

_____

_____

_____

signaling

_____

_____

_____

SOHO

_____

_____

_____

Focus Questions

1. What is a SPID (service profile identifier)?

   _____

   _____

2. What is a TA (terminal adapter)?

   _____

   _____

3. What is TE1 (terminal equipment type 1)?

   _____

   _____

4. What is TE2 (terminal equipment type 2)?

   _____

   _____

5. What is UNI (user-network interface)?

   _____

   _____

6. What is the top speed at which ISDN operates?

   _____

   _____

7. How many B channels does ISDN use?

   _____

   _____

8. How many D channels does ISDN use?

   _____

   _____

9. The ISDN service provider must provide the phone number and what type of identification number?

   _____

   _____

10. Which channel does ISDN use for call setup?

    _____

    _____

11. The school superintendent asks you to explain what ISDN is. She is not an experienced networker, but she is a competent manager. Develop an outline for explaining ISDN to her. Include your opening and closing paragraphs.

_____

_____

12. What are some considerations for providing total control over initial DDR connections?

_____

_____

CCNA Exam Review Questions

The following questions help you review for the CCNA exam. The answers appear in Appendix A, "Answers to CCNA Exam Review Questions."

1. At the central site, what device can provide the connection for dialup access?

    A.   Switch

    B.   Router

    C.   Bridge

    D.   Hub

2. For which of the following locations would ISDN service be inadequate?

    A.   A large concentration of users at a site

    B.   A small office

    C.   A single-user site

    D.   None of the above

3. Protocols that begin with E specify what?

    A.   Telephone network standards

    B.   Switching and signaling

    C.   ISDN concepts

    D.   This is not used with ISDN.

4. If you want to use CHAP for authentication when using ISDN, what protocol should you select?

    A.   HDLC

    B.   SLIP

    C.   PPP

    D.   PAP

5. On a router, which of the following commands do you use to set the ISDN switch type?

    A.   Router> **isdn switch-type**

    B.   Router# **isdn switch-type**

    C.   Router(config-if)# **isdn switch-type**

    D.   Router(config)# **isdn switch-type**

6. Which of the following commands can be used to verify DDR operation? (Choose all that apply.)

A. **show dialer**

B. **show isdn active**

C. **show isdn status**

D. All of the above

Chapter 15

Frame Relay

You learned that PPP and ISDN are two WAN technologies that can be implemented to solve connectivity issues for locations that need access to geographically distant locations. In this chapter, you learn about another type of WAN technology, Frame Relay, that can solve connectivity issues for users who need access to geographically distant locations.

In this chapter, you learn about Frame Relay services, standards, components, and operation. In addition, this chapter describes the configuration tasks for Frame Relay service, along with the commands for monitoring and maintaining a Frame Relay connection.

Concept Questions

Demonstrate your knowledge of these concepts by answering the following questions in the space provided.

1.   List all the data communication equipment needed to implement Frame Relay.

_____

_____

_____

2.   List the router commands needed to implement Frame Relay on the router.

_____

_____

_____

_____

_____

_____

_____

3.   Frame Relay WAN technology provides a flexible method of connecting LANs. Why is this so, and how does it work?

_____

_____

_____

_____

_____

Vocabulary Exercise

Define the following terms as completely as you can. Use the online curriculum or Chapter 15 of the *Cisco Networking Academy Program CCNA 3 and 4 Companion Guide* for help.

BECN

_____
_____
_____

CIR

_____
_____
_____

CPE

_____
_____
_____

DCE

_____
_____
_____

DE

_____
_____
_____

DLCI

_____
_____
_____

DTE

_____
_____
_____

excess burst

_____
_____
_____

FECN

_____
_____
_____

Frame Relay

_____
_____
_____

Frame Relay switch

_____
_____
_____

LMI

_____
_____
_____

local access rate

_____
_____
_____

media

_____

_____

_____

PDN

_____

_____

_____

PVC

_____

_____

_____

VC

_____

_____

_____

CCNA Exam Review Questions

The following questions help you review for the CCNA exam. The answers appear in Appendix A, "Answers to CCNA Exam Review Questions."

1. How does Frame Relay handle multiple conversations on the same physical connection?

    A. It duplexes the conversations.

    B. It multiplexes the circuits.

    C. It converts it to an ATM cell.

    D. Multiple conversations are not allowed.

2. Which of the following protocols does Frame Relay use for error correction?

    A. Physical and data-link protocols

    B. Upper-layer protocols

    C. Lower-layer protocols

    D. Frame Relay does not do error correction.

3. Which of the following does Frame Relay do to make its DLCIs global?

    A. It broadcasts them.

    B. It sends out unicasts.

    C. It sends out multicasts.

    D. DLCIs can't become global.

4. Which of the following is the data rate at which the Frame Relay switch agrees to transfer data?

    A. Committed information rate

    B. Data transfer rate

    C. Timing rate

    D. Baud rate

5. Which of the following assigns DLCI numbers?

    A. The end user

    B. The network root

    C. A DLCI server

    D. The service provider

6. DLCI information is included in which field of the Frame Relay header?

    A. The Flag field

    B. The Address field

    C. The Data field

    D. The Checksum field

7. Which of the following does Frame Relay use to keep PVCs active?

    A. Point-to-point connections

    B. Windows sockets

    C. Keepalives

    D. They become inactive.

8. How does Frame Relay use inverse ARP requests?

    A. It maps IP addresses to MAC addresses.

    B. It maps MAC addresses to IP addresses.

    C. It maps MAC addresses to network addresses.

    D. It uses the IP address-to-DLCI mapping table.

9. Which of the following does Frame Relay use to determine the next hop?

    A. An ARP table

    B. A RIP routing table

    C. A Frame Relay map

    D. An IGRP routing table

10. For which of the following tasks does Frame Relay use split horizon?

    A. To increase router updates

    B. To prevent routing loops

    C. To raise convergence times

    D. Frame Relay does not use split horizon.

Chapter 16

Introduction to Network Administration

Today's network administrators must manage complex wide-area networks (WANs) to support the growing number of software applications that are built around Internet Protocol (IP) and the web. These WANs place a great demand on network resources and require high-performance networking technologies. WANs are environments that incorporate multiple media, multiple protocols, and interconnections to other networks, such as the Internet. Growth and manageability of these network environments are achieved by the often-complex interaction of protocols and features.

Despite improvements in equipment performance and media capabilities, WAN design is becoming more difficult. Carefully designed WANs can reduce problems associated with a growing networking environment. To design reliable, scalable WANs, network designers must keep in mind that each WAN has specific design requirements. This chapter provides an overview of the methodologies used to design WANs.

The first PCs were designed as standalone desktop systems. The operating system (OS) software allowed one user at a time to access files and system resources. The user had physical access to the PC. As PC-based computer networks gained popularity in the workplace, software companies developed specialized network operating systems (NOSs). Developers designed NOSs to provide file security, user privileges, and resource sharing among multiple users. The explosive growth of the Internet compelled developers to build the NOSs of today around Internet-related technologies and services, such as the World Wide Web.

Within a decade, networking has become of central importance to desktop computing. The distinction between modern desktop operating systems, now loaded with networking features and services, and their NOS counterparts has blurred. Now, most popular operating systems, such as Microsoft Windows 2000 and Linux, are found on high-powered network servers and on end users' desktops.

The function of an operating system on a workstation is to control the computer hardware, program execution environment, and user interface. The OS performs these functions for a single user or a number of users who share the machine serially rather than concurrently. An administrator may set up accounts for more than one user, but multiple users cannot log on to the system at the same time.

In contrast, network operating systems distribute their functions over a number of networked computers. A NOS depends on the native OS in each computer. It then adds functions that allow access to shared resources by a number of users concurrently.

Concept Questions

Demonstrate your knowledge of these concepts by answering the following questions in the space provided.

1. Describe the concepts of WAN communication and the two types of switching technologies that are involved.

    _____

    _____

    _____

    _____

    _____

    _____

2. What are the three general factors that the WAN design process must to take into account?

    _____

    _____

    _____

    _____

    _____

    _____

    _____

    _____

    _____

3. Network designs tend to follow one of two general design strategies: mesh or hierarchical. In a mesh structure, the network topology is flat; all routers perform essentially the same functions, and there is usually no clear definition of where specific functions are performed. Expansion of the network tends to proceed in a haphazard, arbitrary manner. In a hierarchical structure, the network is organized in layers, each of which has one or more specific functions. What are some of the benefits of using a hierarchical model?

    _____

    _____

    _____

    _____

    _____

    _____

_____
_____
_____
_____
_____
_____
_____
_____
_____
_____
_____

4.   Describe the client/server model relationship, and provide an example.

_____
_____
_____
_____
_____
_____

5.   Compare and contrast the functions and roles of a networking operating system and a regular workstation operating system.

_____
_____
_____
_____
_____
_____

6.   List and describe some of the driving forces behind network management.

_____
_____
_____
_____
_____

_____
_____
_____
_____
_____
_____
_____

7.   List some of the things a management agent might keep track of.

_____
_____
_____

Vocabulary Exercise

Define the following terms as completely as you can. Use the online curriculum or Chapter 16 of the *Cisco Networking Academy Program CCNA 3 and 4 Companion Guide* for help.

access layer

_____
_____
_____

Alarm group

_____
_____
_____

CIMP

_____
_____
_____

circuit

_____
_____
_____

circuit switching

_____

_____

_____

core layer

_____

_____

_____

dedicated link

_____

_____

_____

distribution layer

_____

_____

_____

Enterprise network

_____

_____

_____

Event group

_____

_____

_____

Filter group

_____

_____

_____

Frame Relay

_____

_____

_____

History group

_____

_____

_____

Host group

_____

_____

_____

Host TopN group

_____

_____

_____

leased line

_____

_____

_____

link

_____

_____

_____

MIB

_____

_____

_____

NMS

_____

_____

_____

Packet Capture group

_____

_____

_____

packet switching

_____

_____

_____

SNMP

_____

_____

_____

Statistics group

_____

_____

_____

T1

_____

_____

_____

T3

_____

_____

_____

WAN link

_____

_____

_____

CCNA Exam Review Questions

The following questions help you review for the CCNA exam. The answers appear in Appendix A, "Answers to CCNA Exam Review Questions."

1. Which of the following are initial concerns in a WAN design? (Choose all that apply.)

   A. Determining whether data outside the company is accessed

   B. Determining who is involved in the design from the customer's standpoint

   C. Determining where shared data resides and who uses it

   D. All of the above

2. When analyzing network load requirements, you should check the worst-case traffic load during what time of the day?

   A. The busiest time

   B. The least-busy time

   C. During network backups

   D. After regular work hours

3. When designing the WAN, where should application servers be placed?

   A. On the enterprise backbone

   B. Close to the users

   C. Near the point of presence

   D. Anyplace the designer chooses

4. Which of the following is *not* a benefit of a hierarchical design model?

   A. Scalability

   B. Ease of implementation

   C. A flat topology

   D. Ease of troubleshooting

5. In most cases, when designing the core layer, what should your main concern be?

   A. Efficient use of bandwidth

   B. Workgroup access

   C. Server placement

   D. Enterprise server placement

6. Which of the following is/are placed on the network backbone?

    A. Server

    B. Routers

    C. Workstations

    D. Application servers

7. Which layer connects users to the LAN?

    A. Workgroup

    B. Core

    C. Access

    D. Distribution

8. Which layer connects a LAN to a WAN link?

    A. Distribution

    B. Workgroup

    C. Core

    D. Access

9. In a one-layer design, the placement of what device becomes extremely important?

    A. Server

    B. Router

    C. Workstation

    D. Switch

10. In a two-layer design, what devices do you use to segment the LAN into individual broadcast domains?

    A. Switches

    B. Routers

    C. Hubs

    D. Repeaters

11.   The campus backbone is typically based on what?

        A.   FDDI

        B.   Token Ring

        C.   Ethernet

        D.   Fast Ethernet

12.   In a hierarchical design, which of the following is a router function?

        A.   Broadcast packets

        B.   Perform bridging

        C.   Perform switching

        D.   Data path decision point

13.   If a server is accessed by more than one workgroup, where should it be placed in a hierarchical design?

        A.   In a workgroup

        B.   At the distribution layer

        C.   At the core layer

        D.   At the access layer

14.   The function of the core layer of the network can best be described as which of the following?

        A.   To provide access to services

        B.   To serve as a distribution point

        C.   To switch packets

        D.   None of the above

15.   What layer provides policy-based connectivity?

        A.   The access layer

        B.   The core layer

        C.   The distribution layer

        D.   All of the above

16. Which of the following is not a part of the OSI and network models?

    A.   Organization

    B.   Information

    C.   Communication

    D.   Feasibility

17. The OSI network management model categorizes five areas of function (sometimes called the FCAPS model). Which of the following options are part of this model?

    A.   Organization

    B.   Fault

    C.   Information

    D.   Security

    E.   Performance

    F.   Communication

    G.   Feasibility

    H.   Configuration

    I.   Accounting

er and the index of refraction.

le.

ptical fiber.

of traditional voice
vice provider's network

uickly, to deliver high-
scalable fail-safe
r-optic technology.
data such as text, video,

ks and the features of
ansmission and their

asic knowledge of some
through materials such
ode and multimode. It
ber optics, and causes of
chnologies: fiber bragg

ET overhead hierarchy,
apter describes how

following questions in

vorks.

optical communication

3.   Explain some of the important design characteristics of fib

_____
_____
_____
_____
_____
_____

4.   List and describe the main components of a fiber-optic ca

_____
_____
_____
_____
_____
_____

5.   Describe the features of multimode fiber.

_____
_____
_____
_____

6.   Describe the features of single-mode fiber.

_____
_____
_____
_____

7.   Describe some ways to obtain the greatest capacity from o

_____
_____
_____
_____
_____
_____

Vocabulary Exercise

Define the following terms as completely as you can. Use the online curriculum or Chapter 17 of the *Cisco Networking Academy Program CCNA 3 and 4 Companion Guide* for help.

FDDI

_____

_____

_____

FDM

_____

_____

_____

IOR

_____

_____

_____

macrobending

_____

_____

_____

MBps

_____

_____

_____

Mbps

_____

_____

_____

microbending

_____

_____

_____

multicast

_____

_____

_____

multiplexing

_____

_____

_____

optical amplifier

_____

_____

_____

PRI

_____

_____

_____

SDH

_____

_____

_____

SONET

_____

_____

_____

statistical multiplexing

---

synchronous transmission

TDM

X.25

CCNA Exam Review Questions

The following questions help you review for the CCNA exam. The answers appear in Appendix A, "Answers to CCNA Exam Review Questions."

1. Which of the following is *not* a key driver of optical networks?

    A. Efficiently meet capacity and scalability requirements in both metropolitan and long-haul network infrastructures

    B. Reduce costs and accelerate profitable new service revenue simultaneously

    C. Reach long distances

    D. Be adaptable through a closed-system architecture

2. Which of the following is true of IOR?

    A. It stands for index of reflection.

    B. It is a light ray bouncing off the interface of two materials.

    C. It is the ratio of the speed of light in a vacuum to the speed of light in a fiber.

    D. Two fibers with different IOR values cannot work together.

3. True or false: Light current is the electrical noise that naturally occurs in the circuit.

    A. True

    B. False

4. Which of the following is *not* a wavelength value used in fiber optics?

    A. 850 nm

    B. 1300 nm

    C. 1450 nm

    D. 1550 nm

5. Which of the following describe(s) fiber optics? (Choose all that apply.)

    A. High-speed transmission

    B. Long transmission distance

    C. More reliability than copper wires

    D. All of the above

6. Which of the following methods can amplify an input optical signal within the fiber?

   A. OA

   B. SONET

   C. ROL

   D. EDFA

7. What is the typical multimode transmission rate?

   A. Hundreds of megabits per second

   B. Hundreds of kilobits per second

   C. Hundreds of gigabits per second

   D. None of the above

8. Which of the following is true of single-mode fiber?

   A. The signal travels through a single-mode fiber at a different rate.

   B. Single-mode fiber has a lower data rate than multimode fiber.

   C. Single-mode fiber allows multimode to travel down the fiber.

   D. Single-mode fiber allows one mode to travel down the fiber.

9. Which of the following are possible problems of the fiber core?

   A. The core can be slightly off center from the cladding center.

   B. The cores might be slightly different sizes.

   C. The core might be noncircular.

   D. All of the above.

10. Which of the following is/are causes of attenuation? (Choose all that apply.)

    A. Scattering

    B. Stress from the manufacturing process

    C. Physical bending

    D. All of the above

11. Which of the following is a *not* a component of fiber-optic cable?

    A. A fiber core

    B. An inner cladding

    C. An outer cladding

    D. A protective outer coating

12. SONET was designed to standardize which of the following?

A. Synchronous networking-enhanced operations, administration, maintenance, and provisioning

B. Asynchronous networking-based operation, administration, maintenance, and provisioning

C. Protections to the SONET facilities at the application layer

D. Transmission standards for ATM

13. Which of the following is *not* one of the three levels of overhead channel for maintenance?

A. SOH

B. COH

C. LOH

D. POH

14. True or false: SONET defines a technology for carrying one signal through a synchronous, flexible, optical hierarchy.

A. True

B. False

15. Which of the following could be a client-side device for a DWDM system?

A. LAN switches

B. Bridges

C. Routers

D. Hubs

16. What device in the DWDM system is used to convert the SONET/SDH-compliant optical signal?

A. Transceiver

B. Transformer

C. Converter

D. Transponder

17. From technical and economic perspectives, what is the most obvious advantage of DWDM technology?

    A. The capability to transmit a lot of data at one time

    B. The capability to provide potentially unlimited transmission capacity

    C. Easy installation

    D. Low cost

18. What are the most compelling technical advantages of DWDM? (Choose all that apply.)

    A. High flexibility

    B. Scalability

    C. High capacity

    D. Transparency

    E. Low maintenance

19. Which of the following does *not* describe metro DWDM?

    A. It is very similar to long-haul DWDM.

    B. It supports subwavelength TDM and wavelength services.

    C. It is driven by demand for fast service provisioning.

    D. It maximizes service density per wavelength.

Chapter 18

Network Management

Now that you have learned how to design and build networks, you can perform tasks such as selecting, installing, and testing cable, as well as determining where wiring closets will be located. However, network design and implementation are only part of what you must know. You also must know how to maintain the network and keep it functioning at an acceptable level. To do this, you must know how to troubleshoot. In addition, you must know when it is necessary to expand or change the network's configuration to meet the changing demands placed on it.

Network management is composed of many different areas, including network documentation, network security, network maintenance, server administration, and server maintenance. This list is not exhaustive, but it is more than enough to cover at this time. Each of the listed topics is just as important as the rest, and none of them should be overlooked.

Many administrators think that, as soon as the network is up and running, their job is over. This couldn't be further from the truth. When a network setup is complete, the real job of a network administrator starts. In this chapter, you learn about managing a network by using techniques such as documenting, monitoring, and troubleshooting.

Documentation

The first, and most critical, component of a good network is documentation. Documentation is the most-talked-about and least-performed task in a network. Documentation represents the network administrator's memory. The following documents assist you in properly documenting your network.

Server and Workstation Configuration Details

Computer Hardware Configuration Worksheet

One Sheet Per Computer

File Server or Workstation:	
Physical Location:	
Make and Model:	
Serial Number:	
Company Invoice Number:	

Removable Media Drives:

Manufacturer	Drive Letter	Capacity	Internal/ External	Internal Drive Bay Number

Fixed Media Drives:

Manufacturer	Drive Letter	Capacity	Internal/ External	Internal Drive Bay Number
Memory Current/Maximum:	Current:		Maximum:	

Peripheral Cards:

Manufacturer	Model	Type	IRQ	DMA	Base Memory Address

Network Interface Cards:

Manufacturer	Node Address	Model	LAN Driver	IRQ	DMA	Base Memory Address
Comments:						

Printer Configuration Worksheet

One Sheet Per Printer

Physical Location:					
Make and Model:					
Serial Number:					
Company Invoice Number:					
Printer ID Number:					
Memory Current/Maximum:	Current:		Maximum:		
Paper Bins	Bin #1 Paper Type		Bin #2 Paper Type		Bin #3 Paper Type
Printer Configuration:					
Serial	Port	Baud Rate	Stop Bits	Parity	Xon/Xoff	Interrupt
Parallel	Port	Polling				Interrupt
Network	IP Address	Polling	MAC Address			
Print Queues:					
Print Operators:					
Comments:					

Software Listings

Computer Software Configuration Worksheet					
One Sheet Per Computer					
Computer Invoice Number:					
Operating System(s):					
Manufacturer:	Version	Service Updates	Network-Capable	Security	
Application Software:					
Manufacturer:	Version	Service Updates	Network-Capable	Installation Directory	Data Directory

Maintenance Records

Computer Repair Worksheet				
One Sheet Per Computer				
Computer Invoice Number:		**Date:**		
Type of Problem:	Hardware		Software	
Problem Description:				
Warranty Coverage:	Yes	No	**Location of Repair:**	
Repair Description:				
Department Charged:				
Authorized By:				
Repair Completed By:				
Comments:				

Security Measures

Network Security Room Form					
One Per Room					

Physical Location:				Date:	
Physical Security:	Door Lock	Windows	False Ceiling	Fire Suppression	Locking Cabinets

Servers Tape Backup:					
Server Name:	Type	Media	Offsite Location	Tape Set Name	Start Day-of-Week
Server #1:					
Server #2:					
Server #3:					

Authorized Access:	Name	Department	Function

Comments:

Network Security User Form

One Per User

Physical Location:			Date:	
Username:			**User ID:**	
Department: Password Length:			Department Manager Home Directory:	
Date ID Expires:			Local Access:	
Access Hours:			Print Access:	
Remote Access:			Administrative Access:	

Inclusive Groups:	Group Name:	Group Rights:	Local/Global:	Restrictions:

Network Duties/Privileges:

Comments:	

Vocabulary Exercise

Define the following terms as completely as you can. Refer to Chapter 18 of the *Cisco Networking Academy Program CCNA 3 and 4 Companion Guide* for help.

backup operations

_____
_____
_____

client/server

_____
_____
_____

connection monitoring

_____
_____
_____

cut sheet diagrams

_____
_____
_____

data recovery

_____
_____
_____

EMI

_____
_____
_____

error report documentation

_____
_____
_____

network access

_____

_____

_____

network baseline, updates, and change verification

_____

_____

_____

network control

_____

_____

_____

network costs

_____

_____

_____

peer-to-peer network

_____

_____

_____

power conditioning

_____

_____

_____

RAID 0

_____

_____

_____

RAID 1

_____

_____

_____

RAID 2

_____

_____

_____

RAID 3

_____

_____

_____

RAID 4

_____

_____

_____

RAID 5

_____

_____

_____

redundancy techniques

_____

_____

_____

RFI

_____

_____

_____

RMON

_____

_____

_____

SNMP

_____

_____

_____

software viruses

_____

_____

_____

static, dust, dirt, and heat

_____

_____

_____

traffic monitoring

_____

_____

_____

Focus Questions

1. What types of network documentation are needed to properly manage a network?

   _____

   _____

   _____

   _____

2. Describe the benefits of network documentation.

   _____

   _____

   _____

   _____

3.   Describe the major components of network security related to network management.

_____
_____
_____

4.   What environmental factors need be considered when managing a network?

_____
_____
_____

5.   Describe the administrator's role in managing networks.

_____
_____
_____

6.   Describe the scientific method of network troubleshooting.

_____
_____
_____
_____
_____
_____
_____
_____
_____
_____
_____

7.   You are discussing network management with a customer. Outline the presentation you would give the customer, explaining network management and how you intend to manage his or her network. Include a script of your opening and closing paragraph.

8. Why is the view of the network important?

    _____

    _____

    _____

9. Why is it necessary to monitor a network?

    _____

    _____

    _____

10. Describe problem solving as it relates to network troubleshooting.

    _____

    _____

    _____

    _____

    _____

11. Describe some troubleshooting methods.

    _____

    _____

    _____

    _____

    _____

12. Describe the administrative side of managing networks.

    _____

    _____

    _____

    _____

    _____

13. Describe some software tools used for network troubleshooting.

    _____

    _____

    _____

CCNA Exam Review Questions

The following questions help you review for the CCNA exam. The answers appear in Appendix A, "Answers to CCNA Exam Review Questions."

1. What type of backup saves only the files that were modified on the same day as the backup operation?

   A. Full backup

   B. Incremental backup

   C. Copy backup

   D. Differential backup

2. RAID 1 features what type of disk redundancy?

   A. Disk striping

   B. Disk backup

   C. Disk duplexing

   D. No redundancy

3. A network baseline is the comparison value that measures what about a network?

   A. Security

   B. Design

   C. Structure

   D. Performance

4. A peer-to-peer network establishes what type of relationship between end stations?

   A. Client-to-client

   B. Client-to-server

   C. Server-to-server

   D. Server-to-Internet

5. What type of file system does Windows NT use for security purposes?

   A. FAT 16

   B. FAT 32

   C. NTFS

   D. NFS

6. A document that shows the physical layout of a building's network wiring is called what?

    A. Cut sheet

    B. Layout diagram

    C. Floor plan

    D. Access list

7. What is the minimum number of drives required for RAID 5?

    A. One

    B. Two

    C. Three

    D. Four

8. In a client/server network, what is it called when a user can access certain files but not others?

    A. User access

    B. User rights

    C. User abilities

    D. User securities

9. What is the IP address of the internal loopback?

    A. 10.10.10.1

    B. 255.255.255.0

    C. 127.0.0.1

    D. 192.0.0.1

10. What is one way to prevent static electricity damage?

    A. Turn off the electricity when working on the computer.

    B. Wear rubber gloves to insulate the equipment.

    C. Use only plastic tools.

    D. Use a grounding strap.

11. What protocol supports network management?

    A. SMTP

    B. NFS

    C. SNMP

    D. FTP

    E. IPX

12. What command shows your IP setting on a Windows NT computer?

    A. **IP**

    B. **IPCONFIG**

    C. **WINIPCFG**

    D. **SHOW IP**

    E. **CONFIG**

13. Which of the following is a method used in network troubleshooting?

    A. Loopback readout

    B. Divide and conquer

    C. Ping of death test

    D. Trace the fault

    E. Reset the server

14. If the server is set up using the Internet Protocol, the clients must use which protocol to communicate with it?

    A. IPX

    B. UDP

    C. IP

    D. Telnet

    E. HTTP

15. What is the most basic form of connection monitoring?

    A. WINIPCFG

    B. Tracert

    C. NetMonitor

    D. LanMeter

    E. Logging on

16. RMON is an extension of what protocol?

    A.   SNMP

    B.   UDP

    C.   IPX

    D.   PING

    E.   SMTP

17. What does the **-n** protocol option stand for in the **ping** command?

    A.   The network number of the ping area

    B.   No repeat

    C.   The number of pings

    D.   Never stop until interrupted

    E.   Nothing

18. How is remote data gathered with RMON?

    A.   Commands

    B.   Tables

    C.   Lists

    D.   Probes

    E.   User interaction

19. The cost of _____ equipment for mission-critical operations needs to be added to the cost of maintaining the network.

    A.   Redundant

    B.   Expensive

    C.   Mechanical

    D.   Security

    E.   Welding

Appendix A

Answers to CCNA Exam Review Questions

Chapter 1

1.   Which OSI layer supports file transfer?

    A.   Application layer

    B.   Network layer

    C.   Presentation layer

    D.   Session layer

    E.   Physical layer

    Answer: A

2.   Which OSI layer negotiates data transfer syntax such as ASCII?

    A.   Network layer

    B.   Transport layer

    C.   Application layer

    D.   Physical layer

    E.   Presentation layer

    Answer: E

3.   Which OSI layer deals with connection coordination between applications?

    A.   Physical layer

    B.   Data link layer

    C.   Transport layer

    D.   Session layer

    E.   Presentation layer

    Answer: D

4.   Which OSI layer supports reliable connections for data transport services?

    A.   Application layer

    B.   Session layer

    C.   Presentation layer

    D.   Physical layer

    E.   Transport layer

    Answer: E

5.   At what layer does routing occur?

    A.   Session layer

    B.   Application layer

    C.   Network layer

    D.   Transport layer

    E.   Data link layer

    Answer: C

Chapter 2

1.   How many bits are in an IP address?

   A.   16

   B.   32

   C.   64

   D.   None of the above

   Answer: B

2.   What is the maximum value of each octet in an IP address?

   A.   128

   B.   255

   C.   256

   D.   None of the above

   Answer: B

3.   The network number plays what part in an IP address?

   A.   It specifies the network to which the host belongs.

   B.   It specifies the identity of the computer on the network.

   C.   It specifies which node on the subnetwork is being addressed.

   D.   It specifies which networks the device can communicate with.

   Answer: A

4.   The host number plays what part in an IP address?

   A.   It designates the identity of the computer on the network.

   B.   It designates which node on the subnetwork is being addressed.

   C.   It designates the network to which the host belongs.

   D.   It designates which hosts the device can communicate with.

   Answer: B

5.   What is the decimal equivalent to the binary number 00101101?

   A.   32

   B.   35

   C.   45

   D.   44

   Answer: C

6.   Convert the decimal number 192.5.34.11 to its binary form.

   A.   11000000.00000101.00100010.00001011

   B.   11000101.01010111.00011000.10111000

   C.   01001011.10010011.00111001.00110111

   D.   11000000.00001010.01000010.00001011

   Answer: A

7.   Convert the binary IP address 1000000.00000101.00100010.00001011 to its decimal form.

   A.   190.4.34.11

   B.   192.4.34.10

   C.   192.4.32.11

   D.   None of the above

   Answer: D

8. What portion of the Class B address 154.19.2.7 is the network address?
   A. 154
   B. 154.19
   C. 154.19.2
   D. 154.19.2.7

   Answer: B

9. Which portion of the IP address 129.219.51.18 represents the network?
   A. 129.219
   B. 129
   C. 129.219.51.0
   D. 129.219.0.0

   Answer: A

10. Which of the following addresses is an example of a broadcast address on the network 123.10.0.0 with a subnet mask of 255.255.0.0?
    A. 123.255.255.255
    B. 123.10.255.255
    C. 123.13.0.0
    D. 123.1.1.1

    Answer: B

11. How many host addresses can be used in a Class C network?
    A. 253
    B. 254
    C. 255
    D. 256

    Answer: B

12. How many subnets can a Class B network have?
    A. 16
    B. 256
    C. 128
    D. None of the above

    Answer: D

13. What is the minimum number of bits that can be borrowed to form a subnet?
    A. 1
    B. 2
    C. 4
    D. None of the above

    Answer: B

14. What is the primary reason for using subnets?
    A. To reduce the size of the collision domain
    B. To increase the number of host addresses
    C. To reduce the size of the broadcast domain
    D. None of the above

    Answer: C

9. What command displays the routes known to a router and how they were learned?

   A. **show ip protocol**

   B. **show ip route**

   C. **show ip ospf**

   D. **show ip ospf neighbor detail**

Answer: B

10. Which of the following are two basic types of dynamic routing?

   A. Static and default

   B. TCP and UDP exchange

   C. Distance vector and link-state

   D. None of the above

Answer: C

11. _____ routing protocols determine the direction and distance to any link in the internetwork; _____ routing protocols are also called shortest path first.

   A. Distance-vector, link-state

   B. Distance-vector, hybrid

   C. Link-state, distance-vector

   D. Dynamic, static

Answer: A

Chapter 4

1. How do you configure automatic redistribution between IGRP and EIGRP?

   A. Configure the two protocols with different AS numbers.

   B. Configure the two protocols with different DS numbers.

   C. Configure the two protocols with the same AS numbers.

   D. Configure the two protocols with the same DS numbers.

Answer: C

2. Which protocol combines the advantages of link-state and distance-vector routing protocols?

   A. RIP

   B. OSPF

   C. IGRP

   D. EIGRP

Answer: D

3. Which algorithm is used to achieve rapid convergence?

   A. Dijkstra's algorithm

   B. Diffusing Update Algorithm

   C. Convergence algorithm

   D. Dual convergence algorithm

Answer: B

4. Which protocol does EIGRP support through the use of protocol-dependent modules (PDMs)?

   A. IS-IS

   B. SNMP

C.   Novell NetWare

D.   DHCP

Answer: C

5.   Which table includes route entries for all destinations that the router has learned and is maintained for each configured routing protocol?

A.   Topology table

B.   Routing table

C.   Neighbor table

D.   Successor table

Answer: B

6.   Which of the following establishes adjacencies in EIGRP?

A.   DUAL finite-state machine

B.   Hello packets

C.   Topology table

D.   Reliable transport protocol

Answer: B

7.   Which of the following guarantees ordered delivery of EIGRP packets to all neighbors?

A   DUAL finite-state machine

B.   Hello packets

C.   Topology table

D.   Reliable transport protocol

Answer: D

8.   What does DUAL do after it tracks all routes, compares them, and guarantees that they are loop-free?

A.   Inserts lowest-cost paths into the routing table

B.   Determines the optimal path and advertises it to the neighbor routers using hello packets

C.   Supports other routed protocols through PDMs

D.   Sends a unicast query to the neighboring routers

Answer: A

9.   How does EIGRP prevent routing loops from occurring with external routes?

A.   By rejecting external routes tagged with a router ID identical to their own

B.   By storing the identities of neighbors that are feasible successors

C.   By rejecting all neighboring routers that have an advertised composite metric that is less than a router's best current metric

D.   By storing all neighboring routes that have loops identified in a special table

Answer: D

10.   On higher-bandwidth connections, such as point-to-point serial links or multipoint circuits, how long is the hello interval used by EIGRP?

A.   5 seconds

B.   10 seconds

C.   60 seconds

D.   120 seconds

Answer: A

Chapter 5

1. Which of the following broadcast methods does an Ethernet medium use to transmit data to and receive data from all nodes on the network?

    A.   A packet

    B.   A data frame

    C.   A segment

    D.   A byte at a time

    Answer: B

2. What is the minimum time it takes Ethernet to transmit 1 byte?

    A.   100 ns

    B.   800 ns

    C.   51,200 ns

    D.   800 ms

    Answer: B

3. Which of the following are characteristics of microsegmentation?

    A.   Dedicated paths between sender and receiver hosts

    B.   Multiple traffic paths within the switch

    C.   All traffic is visible on the network segment at once

    D.   A and B

    Answer: D

4. LAN switches are considered to be which of the following?

    A.   Multiport repeaters operating at Layer 1

    B.   Multiport hubs operating at Layer 2

    C.   Multiport routers operating at Layer 3

    D.   Multiport bridges operating at Layer 2

    Answer: D

5. Asymmetric switching is optimized for which of the following?

    A.   Client/server network traffic in which the "fast" switch port is connected to the server

    B.   An even distribution of network traffic

    C.   Switches without memory buffering

    D.   A and B

    Answer: A

6. In _____ switching, the switch checks the destination address and immediately begins forwarding the frame, and in _____ switching, the switch receives the complete frame before forwarding it.

    Λ.   Store-and-forward, symmetric

    B.   Cut-through, store-and-forward

    C.   Store-and-forward, cut-through

    D.   Memory buffering, cut-through

    Answer: B

7. Which of the following is/are likely to cause congestion?

    A.   Internet access

    B.   Central database access

C.   Video and image transmission

D.   All of the above

Answer: D

8.   Which of the following is *not* a cause of excessive broadcasts?

A.   Too many client packets looking for services

B.   Too many server packets announcing services

C.   Too many routing table updates

D.   Too many network segments

Answer: D

9.   A primary data link layer design goal is the selection of _____ devices, such as bridges or LAN switches, used to connect _____ media to form LAN segments.

A.   Layer 3, Layer 2

B.   Layer 1, Layer 2

C.   Layer 2, Layer 1

D.   Layer 2, Layer 3

Answer: C

10.   Which of the following specifications for 10BASE T is wrong?

A.   Data rate is 10 Mbps

B.   Maximum length is 400 meters

C.   Signaling method is baseband

D.   Media is Category 5 UTP

Answer: B

11.   Which of the following are benefits of implementing Layer 3 devices in your LAN?

A.   It allows segmentation of the LAN into unique physical and logical networks.

B.   It filters data-link broadcasts and multicasts and allows for WAN connectivity.

C.   It provides logical structure to the network.

D.   All of the above

Answer: D

Chapter 6

1.   The access layer provides which of the following?

A.   The entry point for users and servers into the network

B.   The point at which all devices connect to the network

C.   All available bandwidth for every user

D.   Always uses switches

Answer: A

2.   The core layer has which of the following characteristics?

A.   It provides as much packet manipulation as possible to ensure security.

B.   It operates as a high-speed switching backbone to forward traffic from one area to another.

C.   Only Layer 2 switches must be used in the core.

D.   It provides multiple pathways to slow down the traffic.

Answer: B

3. Which of the following are benefits of implementing Layer 3 devices in your LAN?

A. Allows segmentation of the LAN into unique physical and logical networks

B. Filters data-link broadcasts and multicasts and allows for WAN connectivity

C. Provides logical structure to the network

D. All of the above

Answer: D

4. What device provides logical segmentation of a LAN?

A. Router

B. Bridge

C. Switch

D. Hub

Answer: A

5. Microsegmentation with switches does which of the following?

A. Creates additional broadcast domains

B. Decreases network segments

C. Creates additional collision domains

D. Creates fewer collision domains

Answer: C

Chapter 7

1. Which of the following are characteristics of microsegmentation?

A. Dedicated paths between sender and receiver hosts

B. Multiple traffic paths within the switch

C. Increased collision domains

D. All of the above

Answer: D

2. How are LAN switches characterized?

A. Multiport repeaters operating at Layer 1

B. Multiport hubs operating at Layer 2

C. Multiport routers operating at Layer 3

D. Multiport bridges operating at Layer 2

Answer: D

3. Asymmetric switching is optimized for which of the following?

A. Client-server network traffic where the "fast" switch port is connected

B. An even distribution of network traffic

C. Switches without memory buffering

D. Load balancing between links

Answer: A

4. In _____ switching, the switch checks the destination address and immediately begins forwarding the frame while in _____ switching the switch receives the complete frame before forwarding it.

A. Store-and-forward;symmetric

B. Cut-through; store-and-forward

C.   Store-and-forward; cut-through

D.   Memory buffering;cut-through

Answer: B

5.   Fragment-free and fast-forward switching are two forms of _____ switching.

      A.   Store-and-forward

      B.   Memory-buffering

      C.   Cut-through

      D.   Symmetric

Answer: C

6.   When connecting a workstation to a switch, what kind of cable do you use?

      A.   Straight-through

      B.   Crossover

      C.   Null-modem

      D.   Standard phone line

Answer: A

7.   Which communication method is characterized by one host sending and one host receiving?

      A.   Broadcast

      B.   Unicast

      C.   Multicast

      D.   None of the above

Answer: B

8.   Which of the following is true of accessing a switch by means of an Ethernet port?

      A.   The console port must be configured first.

      B.   A crossover cable connects the workstation to the switch port.

      C.   The switch can be managed only through the console port.

      D.   The switch must be configured with an IP address.

      E.   None of the above

Answer: D

9.   Which type of cable is used when connecting two switches?

      A.   Straight-through

      B.   Crossover

      C.   Null-modem

      D.   Standard phone line

      E.   Rollover

      F.   Console

Answer: B

10.   Which of the following is true of **set** command-based switches?

      A.   Configuration changes are made in global configuration mode.

      B.   The **copy run start** command is used to save the configuration to NVRAM.

      C.   The **clear config all** command resets the switch to the factory default configuration.

      D.   The privileged mode prompt is Switch#.

Answer: C

11. What are two major classifications of Cisco Catalyst switches?

    A.   Cisco IOS software command-based and **set** command-based

    B.   **set** command-based and menu-driven

    C.   Cisco IOS software command-based and menu-driven

    D.   CLI-based and Cisco IOS software command-based

Answer: A

12. Unlike a router, a switch has only a single IP address. On which interface is this address defined?

    A.   Interface Ethernet 0 on a **set** command-based switch

    B.   Interface sc0 on an IOS command-based switch

    C.   Interface VLAN1 on a **set** command-based switch

    D.   Interface VLAN1 on a Cisco IOS software command-based switch

Answer: D

13. Which of the following best describes the effect of the command **set port speed 10/1 auto**?

    A.   Both the speed and duplex mode of the specified port are automatically negotiated.

    B.   The speed of the first port on module 10 is automatically negotiated.

    C.   Ports operating at 10 Mbps automatically negotiate their duplex mode.

    D.   Ports can negotiate a speed up to 10 times their base rate.

Answer: A

14. What command is used to view the active configuration of a **set** command-based switch?

    A.   **show config**

    B.   **show running-config**

    C.   **show active-config**

    D.   **show current-config**

Answer: A

Chapter 8

1. The goal of redundant topologies is to eliminate network outages caused by how many points of failure?

    A.   One

    B.   Two

    C.   Three

    D.   Four

Answer: A

2. What is the purpose of the Spanning Tree Protocol?

    A.   To maintain single-loop paths

    B.   To maintain a loop-free network

    C.   To maintain a multiloop network

    D.   To maintain a reduced-loop network

Answer: B

3. When the network topology changes, what happens?

    A.   You must initiate a spanning-tree recalculation.

    B.   You must reconfigure the top node of the spanning tree.

    C.   You must reconfigure all devices participating in the spanning tree.

    D.   The Spanning Tree Protocol reconfigures switch or bridge ports automatically.

Answer: D

4. On the root bridge, all ports are what?

    A. Root ports

    B. Blocked ports

    C. Designated ports

    D. Nondesignated ports

    Answer: C

5. How does the Spanning Tree Protocol select the root port on a nonroot bridge?

    A. The root port is the highest-cost path from the nonroot bridge to the root bridge.

    B. The root port is the lowest-cost path from the nonroot bridge to the root bridge.

    C. The root port is the lowest-cost path from the nonroot bridge to the backup root bridge.

    D. The root port is the highest-cost path from the nonroot bridge to the backup root bridge.

    Answer: B

6. Which bridge does the Spanning Tree Protocol select as the root bridge?

    A. The one with the lowest priority

    B. The one with the lowest bridge ID

    C. The one with the highest bridge ID

    D. The one with the highest MAC address

    Answer: B

7. What comprises the Spanning Tree Protocol bridge ID?

    A. Bridge priority and bridge IP address

    B. Bridge priority and bridge MAC address

    C. Bridge MAC address and bridge IP address

    D. Bridge MAC address and Ethernet port number

    Answer: B

8. In what state can a port populate its MAC address table but not forward user frames?

    A. Learning state

    B. Blocking state

    C. Listening state

    D. Forwarding state

    Answer: A

9. In the revised IEEE specification, what is the cost of a 100-Mbps link?

    A. 4

    B. 10

    C. 19

    D. 100

    Answer: C

10. What is the definition of convergence for the Spanning Tree Protocol?

    A. All the ports have transitioned to the blocking state.

    B. All the ports have transitioned to the forwarding state.

    C. All the ports have transitioned to either the forwarding or listening state.

    D. All the ports have transitioned to either the forwarding or blocking state.

    Answer: D

11. What is the default max_age for the Spanning Tree Protocol?
    A. 2 seconds
    B. 15 seconds
    C. 20 seconds
    D. 30 seconds
    Answer: C

12. What Rapid Spanning Tree Protocol state is equivalent to the Spanning Tree Protocol blocking state?
    A. Blocking
    B. Dropping
    C. Discarding
    D. Forwarding
    Answer: C

13. What port role specifies a forwarding port elected for every switched LAN segment when using the Rapid Spanning Tree Protocol?
    A. Root
    B. Backup
    C. Alternate
    D. Designated
    Answer: D

14. How does the STP provide a loop-free network?
    A. By placing all ports in the blocking state
    B. By placing all bridges in the blocking state
    C. By placing some ports in the blocking state
    D. By placing all bridges in the forwarding state
    Answer: C

Chapter 9

1. What does the phrase *microsegmentation with scalability* mean?
    A. The ability to enlarge networks without creating collision domains
    B. The ability to put a huge number hosts on one switch
    C. The ability to broadcast to more nodes at once
    D. All of the above
    Answer: A

2. Switches, as the core element of VLANs, provide the intelligence to do which of the following?
    A. Group users, ports, or logical addresses into a VLAN
    B. Make filtering and forwarding decisions
    C. Communicate with other switches and routers
    D. All of the above
    Answer: D

3. Each _____ segment connected to a _____ port can be assigned to only one VLAN.
    A. Switch, hub
    B. Hub, router

C.   Hub, switch

D.   LAN, hub

Answer: C

4.   Which of the following is *not* an advantage of using static VLANs?

A.   They are secure.

B.   They are easy to configure.

C.   They are easy to monitor.

D.   They automatically configure ports when new stations are added.

Answer: D

5.   Which of the following is *not* a criterion on which VLANs can be based?

A.   Port ID and MAC address

B.   Protocol

C.   Application

D.   All of the above are criteria on which VLANs can be based.

Answer: D

6.   Which of the following is *not* a beneficial effect of adding a VLAN?

A.   Switches do not need to be configured.

B.   Broadcasts can be controlled.

C.   Confidential data can be protected.

D.   Physical boundaries that prevent user groupings can be removed.

Answer: A

Chapter 10

1.   What is the primary advantage of using a trunk link?

A.   It provides more bandwidth for each trunk.

B.   It reduces router and switch ports.

C.   It allows for a single VLAN on each physical port.

D.   It creates less overhead on the router.

Answer: B

2.   What protocol is Cisco-proprietary and is designed to carry traffic from multiple VLANs?

A.   802.11A

B.   802.1Q

C.   VNET

D.   ISL

Answer: D

3.   VTP messages are encapsulated in either Cisco-proprietary Inter-Switch Link (ISL) or what type of frame?

A.   IEEE 802.1D protocol frame

B.   IEEE 802.1R protocol frame

C.   802.11D protocol frame

D.   802.19 protocol frame

Answer: A

4. True or false: Two different versions of VTP can run in your management domain, VTP Version 1 and VTP Version 2. The two versions are interoperable.

    A. True
    B. False

    Answer: B

5. A switch's default behavior is to propagate broadcasts and unknown _____ across the network.

    A. Frames
    B. Packets
    C. Tags
    D. VLANs

    Answer: B

6. In switched networks, _____ is/are used to provide communication between VLANs.

    A. Route processors
    B. Modulators
    C. VTP
    D. Subnets

    Answer: A

Chapter 11

1. Who or what assigns private addresses?

    A. The network administrator from RFC 1918
    B. American Registry for Internet Numbers (ARIN)
    C. Réseaux IP Européennes (RIPE)
    D. Any address can be a private address

    Answer: A

2. Which of the following are valid RFC 1918 private addresses? (Choose all that apply.)

    A. 10.0.0.0/8
    B. 192.168.0.0/16
    C. 172.16.0.0/12
    D. All of the above

    Answer: D

3. The BOX company maintains its own public web server, and it is about to implement NAT. Which type of NAT will be used for the web server?

    A. Dynamic
    B. Static
    C. PAT
    D. No NAT at all

    Answer: B

4. Which type of NAT will be used for the CEO workstation in the BOX company?

    A. Dynamic
    B. Static
    C. PAT
    D. No NAT at all

    Answer: D

5.   Which of the following applications does Cisco IOS NAT support? (Choose all that apply.)

        A.   ICMP

        B.   DNS zone transfers

        C.   BootP

        D.   File Transfer Protocol (FTP) (including PORT and PASV)

Answer: A, D

6.   Which of the following traffic types does Cisco IOS NAT not support? (Choose all that apply.)

        A.   ICMP

        B.   DNS zone transfers

        C.   BootP

        D.   File Transfer Protocol (FTP) (including PORT and PASV)

Answer: B, C

7.   BootP supports _____, and DHCP supports _____.

        A.   Static mapping, dynamic mapping

        B.   PAT, NAT

        C.   RTP, PAT

        D.   NAT, DHCP

Answer: A

8.   What is the order of DHCP messages?

        A.   DHCPACK, DHCPOFFER, DHCPREQUEST, DHCPDISCOVER

        B.   DHCPREQUEST, DHCPACK, DHCPDISCOVER, DHCPOFFER

        C.   DHCPOFFER, DHCPDISCOVER, DHCPREQUEST, DHCPACK

        D.   DHCPDISCOVER, DHCPOFFER, DHCPREQUEST, DHCPACK

Answer: D

Chapter 12

1.   Which of the following statements pertaining to ISDN is true?

        A.   The ISDN BRI offers two B channels and one D channel.

        B.   The D channel, operating at 16 Kbps, is meant to carry user data.

        C.   The ISDN BRI offers 23 B channels and one D channel in North America.

        D.   The total bit rate of the ISDN BRI is 2.533 Mbps.

Answer: A

2.   Which of the following statements is *not* true of ATM technology?

        A.   It can transfer voice, video, and data.

        B.   ATM offers higher bandwidth than Frame Relay.

        C.   It has a cell-based architecture rather than a frame-based architecture.

        D.   ATM cells are always a fixed length of 35 bytes.

Answer: D

3.   What is equipment on a subscriber's premises that connects to a service provider's central office called?

        A.   DTE

        B.   DCE

        C.   CPE

        D.   None of the above

Answer: C

4. Which of the following is *not* a circuit-switched connection?
    A. SONET
    B. Plain Old Telephone System (POTS)
    C. ISDN Basic Rate Interface (BRI)
    D. ISDN Primary Rate Interface (PRI)

    Answer: A

5. Which of the following is *not* a packet-switched connection?
    A. Frame Relay
    B. X.25
    C. Asynchronous Transfer Mode (ATM)
    D. SONET

    Answer: D

6. ISDN BRI is composed of which of the following?
    A. Two B channels and two D channels
    B. Two B channels and one D channel
    C. 23 B channels and one D channel
    D. 30 B channels and one D channel

    Answer: B

Chapter 13

1. Which of the following is/are the network-layer protocol(s) supported by PPP? (Choose all that apply.)
    A. Novell IPX
    B. TCP/IP
    C. AppleTalk
    D. All of the above

    Answer: D

2. In a PPP frame, what field identifies whether you have encapsulated IPX or TCP/IP?
    A. Flag
    B. Control
    C. Protocol
    D. FCS

    Answer: C

3. When you're running PPP, LCP is responsible for which of the following?
    A. Establishing, maintaining, and terminating the point-to-point connection
    B. Maintaining several links
    C. Router updates
    D. Compression

    Answer: A

4. What type of handshaking occurs when PAP is the selected PPP authentication protocol?
    A. One-way
    B. Two-way
    C. Three-way
    D. Four-way

    Answer: B

5.   What command on the router can you use to check the LCP and NCP states for PPP?

    A.   router> **show interfaces**

    B.   router(config)# **show interfaces**

    C.   router# **show interfaces**

    D.   router(config-if)# **show interfaces**

Answer: C

Chapter 14

1.   At the central site, what device can provide the connection for dialup access?

    A.   Switch

    B.   Router

    C.   Bridge

    D.   Hub

Answer: B

2.   For which of the following locations would ISDN service be inadequate?

    A.   A large concentration of users at a site

    B.   A small office

    C.   A single-user site

    D.   None of the above

Answer: A

3.   Protocols that begin with E specify what?

    A.   Telephone network standards

    B.   Switching and signaling

    C.   ISDN concepts

    D.   This is not used with ISDN.

Answer: A

4.   If you want to use CHAP for authentication when using ISDN, what protocol should you select?

    A.   HDLC

    B.   SLIP

    C.   PPP

    D.   PAP

Answer: C

5.   On a router, which of the following commands do you use to set the ISDN switch type?

    A.   Router> **isdn switch-type**

    B.   Router# **isdn switch-type**

    C.   Router(config-if)# **isdn switch-type**

    D.   Router(config)# **isdn switch-type**

Answer: D

6.   Which of the following commands can be used to verify DDR operation? (Choose all that apply.)

    A.   **show dialer**

    B.   **show isdn active**

    C.   **show isdn status**

    D.   All of the above

Answer: D

Chapter 15

1.   How does Frame Relay handle multiple conversations on the same physical connection?

    A.   It duplexes the conversations.

    B.   It multiplexes the circuits.

    C.   It converts it to an ATM cell.

    D.   Multiple conversations are not allowed.

Answer: B

2.   Which of the following protocols does Frame Relay use for error correction?

    A.   Physical and data-link protocols

    B.   Upper-layer protocols

    C.   Lower-layer protocols

    D.   Frame Relay does not do error correction.

Answer: B

3.   Which of the following does Frame Relay do to make its DLCIs global?

    A.   It broadcasts them.

    B.   It sends out unicasts.

    C.   It sends out multicasts.

    D.   DLCIs can't become global.

Answer: C

4.   Which of the following is the data rate at which the Frame Relay switch agrees to transfer data?

    A.   Committed information rate

    B.   Data transfer rate

    C.   Timing rate

    D.   Baud rate

Answer: A

5.   Which of the following assigns DLCI numbers?

    A.   The end user

    B.   The network root

    C.   A DLCI server

    D.   The service provider

Answer: D

6.   DLCI information is included in which field of the Frame Relay header?

    A.   The Flag field

    B.   The Address field

    C.   The Data field

    D.   The Checksum field

Answer: B

7.   Which of the following does Frame Relay use to keep PVCs active?

    A.   Point-to-point connections

    B.   Windows sockets

    C.   Keepalives

    D.   They become inactive.

Answer: C

8. How does Frame Relay use inverse ARP requests?

   A. It maps IP addresses to MAC addresses.

   B. It maps MAC addresses to IP addresses.

   C. It maps MAC addresses to network addresses.

   D. It uses the IP address-to-DLCI mapping table.

   Answer: D

9. Which of the following does Frame Relay use to determine the next hop?

   A. An ARP table

   B. A RIP routing table

   C. A Frame Relay map

   D. An IGRP routing table

   Answer: C

10. For which of the following tasks does Frame Relay use split horizon?

    A. To increase router updates

    B. To prevent routing loops

    C. To raise convergence times

    D. Frame Relay does not use split horizon.

    Answer: B

Chapter 16

1. Which of the following are initial concerns in a WAN design? (Choose all that apply.)

   A. Determining whether data outside the company is accessed

   B. Determining who is involved in the design from the customer's standpoint

   C. Determining where shared data resides and who uses it

   D. All of the above

   Answer: D

2. When analyzing network load requirements, you should check the worst-case traffic load during what time of the day?

   A. The busiest time

   B. The least-busy time

   C. During network backups

   D. After regular work hours

   Answer: A

3. When designing the WAN, where should application servers be placed?

   A. On the enterprise backbone

   B. Close to the users

   C. Near the point of presence

   D. Anyplace the designer chooses

   Answer: B

4. Which of the following is *not* a benefit of a hierarchical design model?

   A. Scalability

   B. Ease of implementation

C.   A flat topology

D.   Ease of troubleshooting

Answer: C

5.   In most cases, when designing the core layer, what should your main concern be?

A.   Efficient use of bandwidth

B.   Workgroup access

C.   Server placement

D.   Enterprise server placement

Answer: A

6.   Which of the following is/are placed on the network backbone?

A.   Server

B.   Routers

C.   Workstations

D.   Application servers

Answer: B

7.   Which layer connects users to the LAN?

A.   Workgroup

B.   Core

C.   Access

D.   Distribution

Answer: C

8.   Which layer connects a LAN to a WAN link?

A.   Distribution

B.   Workgroup

C.   Core

D.   Access

Answer: D

9.   In a one-layer design, the placement of what device becomes extremely important?

A.   Server

B.   Router

C.   Workstation

D.   Switch

Answer: A

10.   In a two-layer design, what devices do you use to segment the LAN into individual broadcast domains?

A.   Switches

B.   Routers

C.   Hubs

D.   Repeaters

Answer: B

11.   The campus backbone is typically based on what?

A.   FDDI

B.   Token Ring

C. Ethernet

D. Fast Ethernet

Answer: D

12. In a hierarchical design, which of the following is a router function?

A. Broadcast packets

B. Perform bridging

C. Perform switching

D. Data path decision point

Answer: D

13. If a server is accessed by more than one workgroup, where should it be placed in a hierarchical design?

A. In a workgroup

B. At the distribution layer

C. At the core layer

D. At the access layer

Answer: B

14. The function of the core layer of the network can best be described as which of the following?

A. To provide access to services

B. To serve as a distribution point

C. To switch packets

D. None of the above

Answer: C

15. What layer provides policy-based connectivity?

A. The access layer

B. The core layer

C. The distribution layer

D. All of the above

Answer: C

16. Which of the following is not a part of the OSI and network models?

A. Organization

B. Information

C. Communication

D. Feasibility

Answer: D

17. The OSI network management model categorizes five areas of function (sometimes called the FCAPS model). Which of the following options are part of this model?

A. Organization

B. Fault

C. Information

D. Security

E. Performance

F. Communication

G. Feasibility

H. Configuration

I. Accounting

Answer: B, D, E, H, I

Chapter 17

1.	Which of the following is *not* a key driver of optical networks?

A.	Efficiently meet capacity and scalability requirements in both metropolitan and long-haul network infrastructures

B.	Reduce costs and accelerate profitable new service revenue simultaneously

C.	Reach long distances

D.	Be adaptable through a closed-system architecture

Answer: D

2.	Which of the following is true of IOR?

A.	It stands for index of reflection.

B.	It is a light ray bouncing off the interface of two materials.

C.	It is the ratio of the speed of light in a vacuum to the speed of light in a fiber.

D.	Two fibers with different IOR values cannot work together.

Answer: C

3.	True or false: Light current is the electrical noise that naturally occurs in the circuit.

A.	True

B.	False

Answer: B

4.	Which of the following is *not* a wavelength value used in fiber optics?

A.	850 nm

B.	1300 nm

C.	1450 nm

D.	1550 nm

Answer: C

5.	Which of the following describe(s) fiber optics? (Choose all that apply.)

A.	High-speed transmission

B.	Long transmission distance

C.	More reliability than copper wires

D.	All of the above

Answer: D

6.	Which of the following methods can amplify an input optical signal within the fiber?

A.	OA

B.	SONET

C.	ROL

D.	EDFA

Answer: D

7.	What is the typical multimode transmission rate?

A.	Hundreds of megabits per second

B.	Hundreds of kilobits per second

C.	Hundreds of gigabits per second

D.	None of the above

Answer: A

8. Which of the following is true of single-mode fiber?

    A. The signal travels through a single-mode fiber at a different rate.

    B. Single-mode fiber has a lower data rate than multimode fiber.

    C. Single-mode fiber allows multimode to travel down the fiber.

    D. Single-mode fiber allows one mode to travel down the fiber.

    Answer: D

9. Which of the following are possible problems of the fiber core?

    A. The core can be slightly off center from the cladding center.

    B. The cores might be slightly different sizes.

    C. The core might be noncircular.

    D. All of the above.

    Answer: D

10. Which of the following is/are causes of attenuation? (Choose all that apply.)

    A. Scattering

    B. Stress from the manufacturing process

    C. Physical bending

    D. All of the above

    Answer: D

11. Which of the following is a *not* a component of fiber-optic cable?

    A. A fiber core

    B. An inner cladding

    C. An outer cladding

    D. A protective outer coating

    Answer: C

12. SONET was designed to standardize which of the following?

    A. Synchronous networking-enhanced operations, administration, maintenance, and provisioning

    B. Asynchronous networking-based operation, administration, maintenance, and provisioning

    C. Protections to the SONET facilities at the application layer

    D. Transmission standards for ATM

    Answer: A

13. Which of the following is *not* one of the three levels of overhead channel for maintenance?

    A. SOH

    B. COH

    C. LOH

    D. POH

    Answer: B

14. True or false: SONET defines a technology for carrying one signal through a synchronous, flexible, optical hierarchy.

    A. True

    B. False

    Answer: B

15. Which of the following could be a client-side device for a DWDM system?

    A. LAN switches

    B. Bridges

C.   Routers

D.   Hubs

Answer: C

16.   What device in the DWDM system is used to convert the SONET/SDH-compliant optical signal?

A.   Transceiver

B.   Transformer

C.   Converter

D.   Transponder

Answer: D

17.   From technical and economic perspectives, what is the most obvious advantage of DWDM technology?

A.   The capability to transmit a lot of data at one time

B.   The capability to provide potentially unlimited transmission capacity

C.   Easy installation

D.   Low cost

Answer: B

18.   What are the most compelling technical advantages of DWDM? (Choose all that apply.)

A.   High flexibility

B.   Scalability

C.   High capacity

D.   Transparency

E.   Low maintenance

Answer: A, B, D

19.   Which of the following does *not* describe metro DWDM?

A.   It is very similar to long-haul DWDM.

B.   It supports subwavelength TDM and wavelength services.

C.   It is driven by demand for fast service provisioning.

D.   It maximizes service density per wavelength.

Answer: A

Chapter 18

1.   What type of backup saves only the files that were modified on the same day as the backup operation?

A.   Full backup

B.   Incremental backup

C.   Copy backup

D.   Differential backup

Answer: B

2.   RAID 1 features what type of disk redundancy?

A.   Disk striping

B.   Disk backup

C.   Disk duplexing

D.   No redundancy

Answer: C

3. A network baseline is the comparison value that measures what about a network?
    A. Security
    B. Design
    C. Structure
    D. Performance

    Answer: D

4. A peer-to-peer network establishes what type of relationship between end stations?
    A. Client-to-client
    B. Client-to-server
    C. Server-to-server
    D. Server-to-Internet

    Answer: A

5. What type of file system does Windows NT use for security purposes?
    A. FAT 16
    B. FAT 32
    C. NTFS
    D. NFS

    Answer: C

6. A document that shows the physical layout of a building's network wiring is called what?
    A. Cut sheet
    B. Layout diagram
    C. Floor plan
    D. Access list

    Answer: A

7. What is the minimum number of drives required for RAID 5?
    A. One
    B. Two
    C. Three
    D. Four

    Answer: C

8. In a client/server network, what is it called when a user can access certain files but not others?
    A. User access
    B. User rights
    C. User abilities
    D. User securities

    Answer: B

9. What is the IP address of the internal loopback?
    A. 10.10.10.1
    B. 255.255.255.0
    C. 127.0.0.1
    D. 192.0.0.1

    Answer: C

10. What is one way to prevent static electricity damage?
    A. Turn off the electricity when working on the computer.
    B. Wear rubber gloves to insulate the equipment.
    C. Use only plastic tools.
    D. Use a grounding strap.

    Answer: D

11. What protocol supports network management?
    A. SMTP
    B. NFS
    C. SNMP
    D. FTP
    E. IPX

    Answer: C

12. What command shows your IP setting on a Windows NT computer?
    A. **IP**
    B. **IPCONFIG**
    C. **WINIPCFG**
    D. **SHOW IP**
    E. **CONFIG**

    Answer: B

13. Which of the following is a method used in network troubleshooting?
    A. Loopback readout
    B. Divide and conquer
    C. Ping of death test
    D. Trace the fault
    E. Reset the server

    Answer: B

14. If the server is set up using the Internet Protocol, the clients must use which protocol to communicate with it?
    A. IPX
    B. UDP
    C. IP
    D. Telnet
    E. HTTP

    Answer: C

15. What is the most basic form of connection monitoring?
    A. WINIPCFG
    B. Tracert
    C. NetMonitor
    D. LanMeter
    E. Logging on

    Answer: E

16. RMON is an extension of what protocol?
    A. SNMP
    B. UDP

C.   IPX

D.   PING

E.   SMTP

Answer: A

17.   What does the **-n** protocol option stand for in the **ping** command?

A.   The network number of the ping area

B.   No repeat

C.   The number of pings

D.   Never stop until interrupted

E.   Nothing

Answer: C

18.   How is remote data gathered with RMON?

A.   Commands

B.   Tables

C.   Lists

D.   Probes

E.   User interaction

Answer: D

19.   The cost of _____ equipment for mission-critical operations needs to be added to the cost of maintaining the network.

A.   Redundant

B.   Expensive

C.   Mechanical

D.   Security

E.   Welding

Answer: A

Notes